CONTENTS

PREFACE

This book has been written with the food business operator, as opposed to the regulatory lawyer, in mind. The production and sale of food within the European Union (EU) are intensely regulated – a feature that is set to increase as a consequence of the food scares that have bedevilled the EU over the last decade, and the emergence of consumer protection as a principal goal of regulation in this field. Accordingly, there is already a wealth of food legislation – Regulations, Directives and Decisions – that has emanated from Brussels, with much more in the pipeline. However, although EU food law is undoubtedly intricate, it is not necessarily complex, and my primary aim in writing this book has been to simplify it into a more readily digestible form.

I have chosen to tackle the subject matter in the following way. In chapters 2 and 3, I explain in outline how policy is made and applied in the European Union, and the roles played by each of the Brussels institutions in the legislative process. In chapter 4, I consider the principle of the free movement of goods, one of the fundamental freedoms enshrined in the EC Treaty, as it relates to intra-Community trade in food. In chapter 5, I outline the key developments in EU food safety policy, as signalled in the 2000 White Paper on Food Safety, the Commission's bold statement of intent for future regulation in this field, and in the remaining chapters (6 to 12) I consider discrete areas of food regulation. As I mentioned above, I have approached this topic with the food business operator in mind, for it is he or she who bears the greatest burden of coping with the increasing level of regulation. I have therefore sought to set out in the plainest terms in each chapter the principal requirements imposed on operators by the relevant legislation, referring, where necessary, to the Web site of the European Union (*Europa*[1]) for more detailed information.

The Web site of the European Union deserves special mention. In the course of writing this book, I have regularly visited the *Europa* Web site for research purposes and updates. It is something that I urge the reader to do.

---

[1] http://.europa.eu.int

There is little information relating to this subject matter that cannot be found within the labyrinth of its pages, and, in an area of law that is expanding as quickly as this, it is a consistently useful reference point. DG SANCO's (Health and Consumer Protection Directorate General) Web pages can be accessed at http://europa.eu.int/comm/food/index_en.html, from where readers can subscribe to an electronic bulletin service that provides regular updates on key developments and reforms. In addition, the contents of any legislation (and case law) can be downloaded from the *Eur-Lex* legal database (http://europa.eu.int/eur-lex/en/index.html) simply by entering the relevant Regulation/Directive number. The latter facility will be particularly useful should reference need to be made to the detailed provisions of a Regulation or Directive.

Penultimate thoughts: I have used the expression European Union and European Community interchangeably; I bear responsibility for all the research undertaken and contents of the final text, and the law is up-to-date as at August 2002.

Finally, this book is dedicated to my mother and step-father, who was so unwell during its writing, my father and step-mother, and my sister, for their much cherished love and support.

London, October 2002
Paul Hardy
2 Harcourt Buildings
Temple
London
EC4Y 9DB

1.   INTRODUCTION

In the European Union[1] unprecedented waves of public concern following the BSE and dioxin food scares forced food safety to the top of the political agenda when the new Commission took office in 1999. By January 2000, the newly created Health and Consumer Protection DG (known by its French acronym as "DG SANCO"), headed by the former Attorney-General of Ireland, David Byrne, had published a "White Paper on Food Safety."[2] A bold statement of intent, the White Paper introduced an Action Plan of 84 new legislative initiatives for improving the quality and safety of food production in the European Union and aimed to have two-thirds of them implemented by January 2002[3]. It makes clear that food safety is to become the overarching concern of all new food legislation.

1.1   The General Food Law Regulation

Central among these reforms was a proposal for a Regulation laying down a framework of general principles applying to all areas of food law ("from the farm to the table") and establishing an independent food authority. "The General Food Law Regulation"[4] was finally adopted on 21 January 2002. It lays down the legitimate objectives and definitions of food law with the primary aims being to ensure a high level of health protection while at the same time safeguarding the effective functioning of the Single Market. It outlines the Commission's commitment to ensure that food law will be based on high-quality, transparent and independent scientific advice and contains a requirement that only safe food be placed on the market. To this end it envisages the creation of a European Food Safety Authority.[5] The

---

[1] The Member States of the European Union are, in order of accession: France, Germany, Italy, the Netherlands, Belgium, Luxembourg (1957), the United Kingdom, Ireland, Denmark (1973), Greece (1981), Spain, Portugal (1986), Austria, Sweden and Finland (1995).

[2] Com (1999) 719 final

[3] The Annex to the White Paper lists the reforms to be undertaken. It appears in Appendix I to this book.

[4] 178/2002/EC discussed further in chapter 5

[5] The change of name from the European Food Authority to the European Food Safety Authority was agreed by the European Parliament in Strasbourg on 11 December 2001.

primary responsibilities of the authority will be risk assessment and risk communication on food safety issues. It will coordinate the scientific research on food risk undertaken in the Member States and communicate its findings to the public. Risk management – formulating legislation and overseeing a system of effective control - will remain distinct from the authority and within the competence of the Commission. Where appropriate, the precautionary principle on which the Commission has recently adopted an important Communication[6] will be applied to risk management evaluations.

Traceability of food, feed and their ingredients is a key requirement of the Regulation, which establishes the principle of traceability at all stages of the production and distribution chain in the food and feed sectors. These are tough requirements obliging food business operators at every stage in the production and distribution process to keep records of the source and destination of each consignment of foodstuff.

A further key principle is that food safety is a shared responsibility. Feed manufacturers, farmers and food business operators will share the primary responsibility for food safety; national authorities will be expected to monitor and enforce this responsibility through the operation of national surveillance and control systems; and the Commission will concentrate on evaluating the ability of national authorities to deliver these systems through audits and inspections.

1.2   Further Legislative Proposals

The proposals set out in the White Paper are as extensive as they are diverse, and include, *inter alia*, the following further "priority measures", which will be considered in the subsequent chapters of this book:

- a proposal for a Regulation on official food and feed safety controls;
- a proposal amending Regulation 258/97 on novel foods and novel food ingredients;

---

[6] COM (2000) 1

2

- a proposal for a Regulation on hygiene;
- proposals amending Directives 89/107/EEC and 95/2/EC on food additives;
- proposals for Regulations on genetically modified (GM) food and feed and the traceability and labeling of GM-produced foods.
- a proposal amending Directive 79/112/EEC on the labelling, presentation and advertising of foodstuffs.

1.3   Other Emerging Policies

1.3.1   Nutrition

The Commission is formulating a comprehensive policy on nutrition and will present an Action Plan of legislative reform for this purpose in due course. Nutrition is recognised as one of the major determinants of human health. There are major trends in the nutritional field within Member States, such as the high incidence of obesity, which have raised public health concerns and caused the Commission to consider that the promotion of a healthy diet is an increasingly important policy objective. To this end, the provision of nutrient content labelling will be reviewed to ascertain whether it can provide better information to consumers, and widespread scientific research is currently taking place to re-evaluate other nutrition-related policies. Additionally, the Commission is considering developing "Recommendations on European Dietary Guidelines" for consumers within the Community. Commissioner Byrne has consistently stated that there are three interwoven compounds of "good food": safety, quality and nutrition; and nutrition, will be the next component of "good food" to fall under the policy-makers' gaze.

1.3.2 The precautionary principle and consumer protection

In 1999, the Amsterdam Treaty incorporated for the first time within the EC Treaty the need for consumer protection to be integrated into EU policy. Article 153 EC[7], which Commissioner Byrne has described as a "quasi-constitutional obligation", provides as follows:

> "In order to promote the interests of consumers and to ensure a high level of consumer protection, the Community shall contribute to protecting health, safety and economic interests of consumers, as well as promoting their right to information, education, and to organise themselves on order to safeguard their interests."

Accordingly the Commission has recently adopted a Communication[8] on the precautionary principle. It is a key element to its policy on consumer protection. The Commission seeks to apply the principle in cases where scientific evidence is insufficient, inconclusive or uncertain, and where the information available points to unacceptable possible risks to human, animal or plant health and/or the environment. The purpose of defining the principle in a Communication is to place it within a structured approach to the analysis of risk and, as importantly, to stir up debate on its scope within an international context. In the EU's perspective, the precautionary principle forms an inherent part of the management of risk and judging what is an acceptable level of risk is considered to be a political responsibility. However, it is increasingly viewed by other trading partners as a bogus means of trade protectionism – witness, as a recent example, the EU-US trade dispute over hormone-treated meat.[9] The Commission's policy is therefore to attempt to achieve as soon as possible some form of consensus on the role and application of the precautionary principle within the multilateral framework of international trade.

---

[7] "EC" is the uniform reference for the EC Treaty
[8] COM (2000) 1
[9] Discussed in further detail in Chapter 12

1.4 Enlargement

The EU is about to enlarge eastwards. Negotiations have been taking place with thirteen candidate countries[10] with the expectation of first accessions taking place before the European Parliament elections in June 2004. Enlargement of a Union to over twenty-five Member States will inevitably change the nature of the EU and sorely test its decision-making capacity. The Treaty of Nice signed in December 2000 has already introduced fundamental procedural modifications to the working of the Commission, the Council, the Parliament, the Court of Justice and the Court of First Instance with a view to easing the decision-making process in an enlarged Union. These reforms will come into force from 2004 onwards[11].

1.5 Conclusion

The White Paper on Food Safety has heralded the most far-reaching overhaul of EU food law since the creation of the European Economic Community in 1957. It is intended to overcome the crisis in consumer confidence that has been caused, and continues to be caused, by a succession of food scares within the Community. Whether it will succeed or not is not within the purview of this book. What, though, can be stated with greater certainty is that the regulatory demands that will be placed on food business operators will be hugely increased by these reforms, a consideration that, in the policy-maker's view, takes second place to the needs of the consumer.

As this book will show, the focus of EU food law has changed from overseeing the free movement of goods within the Single Market to ensuring that only safe food is marketed. The following chapters will consider the basic foundations of EU law and the roles of the Community institutions before turning to concentrate on the essential reforms taking place in EU

---

[10] Slovenia; Czech Republic; Cyprus; Slovakia; Hungary; Malta; Poland; Estonia; Romania; Lithuania; Latvia; Bulgaria and Turkey.
[11] That said, Ireland has decided by referendum not to ratify the Treaty of Nice

food law. As mentioned in the preface, readers of this book are encouraged to refer to the DG SANCO's Web site for regular updates. This is, to say the least, a fast-moving area of law.

2. IMPLEMENTATION OF EUROPEAN UNION POLICY

The principal mechanism for implementing European Union policy in the 15 Member States is through directly effective legislation, which Member States are obliged to transpose into national law.

2.1   Types of Community Legislation

2.1.1   *Primary legislation*

2.1.1.1   *The EC Treaties*

The EC Treaty is the primary source of the supranational jurisdiction of the European Community over Member States. It has been described as the *de facto* constitution of the European Community; it defines the boundaries of its competence to act.[1] Although commonly described as the EC Treaty, it is in fact a consolidation of the original EEC Treaty, which was signed in 1957 in Rome by the founding members Germany, France, Italy and the Benelux countries, and which created the European Economic Community, as amended by the 1986 Single European Act, the 1992 Treaty on European Union (the Treaty of Maastricht), which created the European Union, and the 1999 Treaty of Amsterdam. Further amendments to the EC Treaty will be introduced by the 2000 Treaty of Nice, which is currently being ratified by Member States.

The European Court of Justice ("ECJ") has held that the fundamental aims of the EC Treaty, so long as they are clearly, precisely and unconditionally expressed within it, are capable of having "direct effect". Direct effect in this context means that they directly impose obligations on both Member States and their citizens, but also confer legally enforceable rights on citizens. In this regard, some provisions of the Treaty can be relied upon by individuals against the actions of Member States or other individuals, and as such are said to have both vertical and horizontal effect.

---

[1] Article 5 EC provides as follows: "The Community shall act within the limits of the powers conferred upon it by this Treaty and of the objectives assigned to it therein."

Direct effect is a significant doctrine of EC law. It was first established by the ECJ in its ground-breaking judgment in *Van Gend en Loos v Nederlanse Administratie der Berlastingen.*[2] The Court held: "The conclusion to be drawn [...] is that the Community constitutes a new legal order of international law for the benefit of which the states have limited their sovereign rights, albeit within limited fields, and the subjects of which comprise not only Member States but also their nationals. Independently of the legislation of Member States, Community law therefore not only imposes obligations on individuals but is also intended to confer upon them rights which become part of their legal heritage. These rights arise not only where they are expressly granted by the Treaty, but also by reason of obligations which the Treaty imposes in a clearly defined way upon individuals as well as upon the Member States and upon the institutions of the Community."

Provisions of the Treaty that have been held to have direct effect include, *inter alia*, equal pay for men and women, freedom to provide services, free movement of workers, free movement of goods and the competition (anti-trust) rules.

2.1.2 Secondary legislation

Article 249 EC[3] provides for the adoption of secondary legislation: "In order to carry out their task and in accordance with the provisions of the Treaty, the European Parliament, acting jointly with the Council and Commission, shall make regulations and issue directives, take decisions, make recommendations or deliver opinions."

2.1.2.1 Regulations

"A regulation shall have general application. It shall be binding in its entirety and directly applicable in all Member States."[4]

---

[2] Case C-26/62
[3] The 1999 Treaty of Amsterdam renumbered the articles of the EC treaty from 1 May 1999 since when the correct citation for articles of the EC Treaty is simply the article number followed by "EC".
[4] Article 249 EC

The phrase "directly applicable" in the context of regulations has been given a two-fold meaning. It certifies that a regulation does not have to await national ratification before it is enforceable in national courts: it is validly enacted and binding from the date specified in its publication in the *Official Journal* of the European Communities. As such, a regulation is said (as with certain EC Treaty provisions) to have direct (vertical) effect. It also certifies that a regulation may be capable of being relied upon by an individual in a national court against the actions of Member States or other individuals. As such, a regulation (as with certain Treaty provisions) may have horizontal effect.

2.1.2.2 Directives

"A directive shall be binding in its entirety upon those to whom it is addressed."[5]

A directive is binding as to the result to be achieved upon each Member State to which it is addressed, but leaves to the national authorities concerned the choice of form and method. Although a directive is a legislative mechanism that affords greater discretion to the legislatures of the Member States, directives have nonetheless been held by the European Court of Justice ("ECJ") to have direct (vertical) effect, as long as they impose clear and precise obligations. This means, for example, that citizens can rely on them when challenging the legality of the conduct of public bodies. They cannot, however, be relied upon in challenging the actions of other individuals and so are not horizontally effective. That said, once a directive has been correctly transposed into national legislation, litigants will no longer have to rely on the direct effect of a Community implementing measure.

The expression "framework directive" is used to signify a directive that identifies policy objectives over a broad field and which is intended to be supplemented by additional, more specific objectives.

---

[5] Article 249 EC

2.1.2.3   Decisions

"A decision shall be binding in its entirety upon those to whom it is addressed."[6]

Decisions take effect when notified to the addressee. They are commonly used by the Commission as a means of imposing penalties for breaches of EC law. If sufficiently precise and clear, decisions are directly effective.

2.1.2.4   Recommendations, opinions, action programmes and communications

These measures are non-binding and therefore have no legal force. They are, however, regularly used by the Community institutions as a means of expressing policy priorities.

2.1.3   Judgements of the EC courts[7]

"The Court of Justice shall ensure that in the interpretation of this Treaty the law is observed" (Article 220 EC).

Through its supervisory responsibility the ECJ has exerted great influence over the application of the EC Treaty and the development of general principles of EC law.

2.2   Application of Community Legislation and Fundamental Principles of Community Law

2.2.1   Giving effect to Community legislation

Member States are required to transpose regulations and directives into their own national legislation within given time periods. Failure to do so can lead to enforcement proceedings being taken against them by the Commission or another Member State under Articles 226 and 227 EC. Once fully transposed, the activity that the regulation or directive sought to regulate becomes a matter of national law.

---

[6] Article 249 EC
[7] The European Court of Justice (ECJ) and Court of First Instance (CFI), both located in Luxembourg

2.2.2   Supremacy

National courts are required to apply Community legislation over and above co-existing national law. Incompatible national legislation is overridden by the supremacy of Community law.[7]

2.2.3   Remedies in national courts

The Community has not created a harmonised system of remedies for breach of Community law. Remedies are therefore left to the jurisdiction of the national courts of Member States with the consequence that they may vary widely.

2.2.4   Subsidiarity

The Treaty of Maastricht incorporated a clause concerning subsidiarity into the EC Treaty. Article 5 EC provides:

> "In areas which do not fall within its exclusive competence, the Community shall take action, in accordance with the principle of subsidiarity, only if and insofar as the objectives of the proposed action cannot be sufficiently achieved by the Member States and can therefore, by reason of the scale of effects of the proposed action, be better achieved by the Community."

Difficult to define in practice, subsidiarity is the principle that decisions should be taken at the level closest to those who are to be affected by them. It was introduced into the Treaty as a sop to those Member States which feared the EU's increasing hegemony over their domestic affairs. A similar provision is found in the Tenth Amendment to the United States Constitution and in Article 30 of the German Constitution.

What falls within the Community's exclusive competence is not clearly defined. The general view is that an activity falls within this definition if the

---

[8]   See for a clear statement of this principle the judgement of the ECJ in *Costa v ENEL* (C-6/64)

Treaties impose on the Community a duty to act. Such areas would include the free movement of goods, persons, services and capital ("the four freedoms"); the Common Commercial Policy; the Common Agricultural Policy; the rules on competition, the common organisation of fisheries; and transport policy. However, in newer areas of EU policy, such as the environment and consumer protection, the Community's jurisdiction is more circumscribed; accordingly, Article 5 might apply. But the wording gives no guidance on how to assess whether an objective "might be better achieved by the Community", and it is the reliance on essentially subjective judgements that is at the root of the legal difficulties posed by the subsidiarity clause.

It is still unclear how subsidiarity will influence Community legislation in the longer term, and whether it will be successfully invoked by Member States to keep the EU institutions in check. Much will depend on the case law developed by the ECJ. It is considered unlikely, however, that Community legislation that is aimed at achieving a legitimate Community-wide objective will ever be overturned for infringing Article 5.

2.2.5   Proportionality

Article 5 EC provides that: "Any action by the Community shall not go beyond what is necessary to achieve the objectives of this Treaty."

Proportionality is a fundamental principle of Community law that has been developed by the ECJ. It requires that the means adopted to achieve an objective correspond to the importance of that objective and are necessary for the achievement of that objective. A common way of describing its effect is that one "must not use a sledgehammer to crack a nut, if a nutcracker will do as well." Proportionality can be relied upon to challenge excessive actions of the Community institutions and Member States.

2.3   Conclusions

Community legislation is the principal means by which Community policy is uniformly applied within the EU. The Commission, the Council of Ministers and the European Parliament each play a significant part in the formulation of legislation. Their roles are examined in the next chapter.

3.   ROLE OF THE EUROPEAN INSTITUTIONS

3.1   European Commission ("the Commission")

3.1.1   Composition

The Commission[1] consists of 20 Commissioners appointed for a term of 5 years; of these, two are appointed from Germany, France, Spain, the United Kingdom and Italy, and one from each of the other Member States. The Commissioners are not selected to represent the interests of their individual Member States; they must be "completely independent in the performance of their duties" (Article 213 EC). The Commission must always act in what it considers to be the Community's best interest.

The Commission is currently undergoing "root and branch" reforms in the wake of the resignation of the Santer Commission in 1999 arising from allegations of fraud and mis-management of the Community budget. One of the most noticeable changes is that Directorates-General ("DGs") are now known by their policy portfolios rather than their numbers. In addition, the following new DGs and Services have been created: the Press and Communication Service; Health and Consumer Protection DG; Enterprise DG; Education and Culture DG; Justice and Home Affairs DG; External Relations DG; Trade DG; Development DG; and Enlargement DG. Each Commissioner is allocated an area of responsibility (see Table 3.I).

---

[1] The Commission's Web site address is http://europa.eu.int/comm

TABLE 3.I
Commissioners and Directorates-General

COMMISSIONER	DIRECTORATES GENERAL AND SERVICES	COMMISSIONER	DIRECTORATES GENERAL AND SERVICES
ROMANO PRODI (PRESIDENT) (ITALY)	Secretariat General Legal Service Press and Information Service	ERKKI LIKANEN (FINLAND)	Information Society DG Enterprise DG
NEIL KINNOCK (VICE PRESIDENT) (UK)	Personnel and Administration DG	MARIO MONTI (ITALY)	Competition DG
LOYOLA DE PALACIO DEL VALLE LERSUNDI (VICE PRESIDENT) (SPAIN)	Transport DG Energy DG	POUL NEILSON (DENMARK)	Development DG European Community Humanitarian Office
MICHEL BARNIER (FRANCE)	Regional Policy DG	CHRIS PATTEN (UK)	External Relations DG Common Service for External Relations
FRITS BOLKESTEIN (NETHERLANDS)	Internal Market DG Customs and Taxation DG	VIVIANE REDING (LUXEMBOURG)	Education and Culture DG Publications Office
PHILLIPPE BUSQUIN (BELGIUM)	Research DG Joint Research Centre	MICHAELE SCHREYER (GERMANY)	Budget DG Financial Control DG Fraud Prevention Office
DAVID BYRNE (IRELAND)	Health and Consumer Protection DG	PEDRO SOLBES MIRA (SPAIN)	Economic and Financial Affairs DG
ANNA DIAMANTOPOULOU (GREECE)	Employment and Social Affairs DG	GUNTHER VERHEUGEN (GERMANY)	Enlargement Service
FRANZ FISHLER (AUSTRIA)	Agriculture DG Fisheries DG	ANTONIO VITORINO (PORTUGAL)	Justice and Home Affairs DG
PASCAL LAMY (FRANCE)	Trade DG	MARGOT WALLSTROM (SWEDEN)	Environment DG

The Commission is headed by a President and two Vice Presidents and works under "the political guidance of its President" (Article 219 EC). The President therefore plays an influential role in the management of the Commission and in its inter-institutional and international relationships. However, the Commission can only take a decision by agreement of a simple majority of its 20 members. It is staffed by international civil servants ("fonctionnaires"), who are all citizens of Member States and who are recruited through public examination.

3.1.2   Functions

The Commission has four main functions.

3.1.2.1   The right of initiative

The Commission is responsible for initiating Community policy and legislation. This is its most significant role. It is also required to participate in the shaping of legislative measures taken by the Council of Ministers ("the Council") and the European Parliament ("the Parliament") "in order to ensure the proper functioning and development of the common market" (Article 211 EC). Additionally, the Council and Parliament – albeit less frequently - may also ask the Commission to make proposals for legislation; but it is the Commission that proposes the great majority of Community legislation. As such, the Commission is rightly considered to have been the driving force behind European integration.[2]

Before it issues a draft proposal for legislation, the Commission will consult widely with representatives of governments, industry, trade unions, special interests groups and its own expert advisory committees. The results of the consultation procedure are then formulated into a draft proposal, which is sent to the Council and the Parliament for their agreement. Once

---

[2] It must, however, be clearly understood that, although it proposes policy and legislation, the Commission is not generally empowered to take executive decisions on EU policies. Such action rests with the Council of Ministers, which is considered more democratically accountable to the citizens of the EU.

the legislative process between the Council and Parliament, in which the Commission fully participates, has been completed and the final legislative act adopted, the Commission becomes responsible for overseeing the Community-wide implementation of the adopted act. In so doing, its role changes from initiator of legislation to watchdog.

3.1.2.2 Watchdog

The Commission is the guardian of the EC Treaties. It monitors the Member States' implementation of primary and secondary Community legislation and brings "infringement" proceedings against Member States in the event of a failure to fulfil an obligation under Community law (Article 226 EC). Should the Member State in question fail to comply with a "reasoned opinion" delivered by the Commission, the matter can be referred to the European Court of Justice ("ECJ") for adjudication and the Member State fined. It also has the power to fine companies indulging in anti-competitive behaviour and to impose provisional dumping duties on products dumped onto the Community market by third countries.

The considerable time taken to bring infringement proceedings and enforce the subsequent judgement of the ECJ allows, in practice, Member States to take advantage of breaches of the rule of Community law with impunity and has attracted much criticism. A recent example is the decision of the ECJ in *Commission v France*.[3] The Court held that France's refusal to permit the selling of British bovine products subject to an approved date-based export scheme was an infringement of Commission decisions authorising the partial lifting of the ban on the export of British beef in the wake of the BSE crisis. The date for lifting the ban was set for 1 August 1999; the Court delivered its judgement concluding that France had infringed its legal obligations under Community law on 13 December 2001, over 2 years later.

---

[3] Case C- 1/00

Furthermore, individuals, corporations and Member States alike may complain to the Commission over the infringement of Community law by a Member State. The Commission, as watchdog, is thus responsible for ensuring that EU policies expressed through legal instruments are uniformly applied.

3.1.2.3   *Executive power*

The Commission performs a limited executive function. It has regulatory powers to ensure that the objectives of the Treaty are achieved (for example proposing regulations and directives and taking decisions), all of which are legally binding. It is also responsible for formulating recommendations and delivering opinions on Community policy. Although the latter are not legally binding, they are commonly and effectively used as a means of indicating the direction of future policy.

Whilst the majority of the application of Community rules is left to the competent authorities of the Member States, there are notable exceptions. For example, the Commission acts as an administrative competition (anti-trust) authority within the jurisdiction of the EU, with the power to approve or reject mergers and acquisitions whose combined market share or value exceed the Commission threshold. It also has the power to fine offending companies heavily for infringements of the competition rules. In addition, the Commission is responsible for the EU's external relations, including trade relations. As such, it represents the EU in international organisations, such as the World Trade Organisation (WTO). It is also responsible for negotiating international agreements with international organisations, trading pacts and third countries, including accession treaties with applicant countries for membership of the EU. Its power to act autonomously in these fields either derives from the EC Treaty or is delegated by the Council.

Lastly, as part of its executive functions, the Commission is responsible for management of the EU budget and Structural Funds.

3.1.2.4   Mediator

The Commission represents the interests of the Community in dealings with the other Community institutions. This is an important function. Article 211 EC provides that the Commission "shall participate in the shaping of measures taken by the Council and the European Parliament in the manner provided for in the Treaty." In negotiations within the Council, where the interests of individual Member States often make agreement difficult to attain, Commission representatives are present in order to assist in achieving consensus and to ensure that the perceived Community interest is not overly compromised by the reluctance of individual Member States. In practice, the Commission can play a pivotal role as mediator in such circumstances. Its institutional knowledge of the evolution of the proposals being discussed and of the amount of national support a draft policy has received means that it can often propose trade-offs or compromises that are more likely to overcome the concerns of Member States.

3.2   Council of Ministers ("the Council")

3.2.1   *Composition*[4]

The Council of Ministers[5] consists of a representative "of each Member State at a ministerial level, authorised to commit the government of that Member State" (Article 203 EC). As such, it is the institution that represents the interests of the governments of the Member States at Community level. It has both executive and legislative powers. Its primary function is to act as the main executive decision-making body of the European Union. It is also, increasingly in co-operation with the Parliament, the legislature of the EU.

---

[4] It is important to distinguish the Council of Ministers from the European Council. The European Council is not a formal institution of the EU. It is composed of the heads of government and foreign ministers of each Member State and the President of the Commission. It meets at least twice a year at "European summits", often at the end of the 6-month term of presidency of the Council. Its meetings are chaired by the President of the Council and focus on the strategic direction of EU policy. In practice, such meetings serve the additional purpose of negotiating agreement on proposals that had failed to attract the necessary majority in the Council of Ministers.

[5] The Council's Web site address is: http//ue.eu.int

In practice, the composition of the Council will depend on the subject matter of the debate. "Agricultural councils", for example, are attended by the agriculture ministers from each Member State. Food-related issues might be dealt with by agriculture, consumer protection, or internal market councils (there are over 20 separate councils). Each year, there are approximately 80 meetings held by the Council, the majority of which take place in Brussels. The meetings are chaired by the relevant minister of the Member State that is holding the Presidency of the Council; in addition to ministers, they are attended by members of the Commission and diplomatic and/or other national government representatives from each Member State.

3.2.2 Presidency

The Presidency of the Council is held in rotation by each Member State for 6 months. It is an influential position to hold. The Presidency will usually arrange and chair all Council meetings and represent the Council in its external dealings. The chair of each Council will be able to set the agenda; by so doing, he may set legislative priorities that are not shared by other Member States. Increasingly the Presidency will liaise with the Presidents of the Commission and the Parliament when formulating legislation as required by the co-decision procedure (see paragraph 3.3.1.2, p23). The Presidency will also play a key role in attempting to obtain majority agreement in Council meetings.

3.2.3 Supporting committees

The Council is supported in its workload by the Committee of Permanent Representatives, better known by its acronym COREPER. The Permanent Representatives are the Heads of each Member State's delegation to the EU and its members are civil servants appointed by the national governments of the Member States. Members of COREPER will attend Council meetings as advisers to their respective ministers. Permanent Representatives are the most important link between Member States and the EU: they are in constant contact with the Commission and the Permanent Representatives of other EU delegations, as well as their own governments.

In statutory terms, COREPER is "responsible for preparing the work of the Council and for carrying out the tasks assigned to it by the Council" (Article 207 EC). However, in practice, COREPER plays a far more influential role in the legislative work of the Council. It is ideally placed to evaluate proposals from the Commission; it helps set the agenda for Council meetings; and it provides much needed continuity to each of the Council's meetings.

COREPER is in turn supported by 200 or so working groups, each comprising national experts from Member States and a member of the Commission. They are the lifeblood of the Council. They examine proposals from the Commission and prepare a report for each, in which they indicate areas of disagreement. It is these areas that are then debated in COREPER meetings.

3.2.4   Functions

The Council has five principal powers.

- It amends and adopts (ratifies) the legislative proposals of the Commission, increasingly in association with the Parliament. (The EU may adopt legislation in one of three ways: through the consultation procedure; through the co-decision procedure; and through the assent procedure. Co-decision is the procedure used to adopt legislation in the field of food regulation and consumer protection.)

- It takes executive decisions.

- It can trigger legislative initiatives by requesting the Commission to undertake studies that the Council considers desirable for the attainment of common objectives. This power is sometimes used when the Council Presidency has a particular legislative agenda that it wants to see initiated during its 6-month term.

- It can delegate the power to make regulations to the Commission when enactment is required urgently.

- It can conclude inter-institutional agreements that serve as the basis for further development of legal principles as in, for example, the Inter-Institutional Agreement on Subsidiarity.

3.2.5 Voting

The Council may act in one of three ways: by simple majority; by qualified majority; or by unanimity. The requirement for unanimity has been greatly reduced by the Single European Act and the Maastricht Treaty and is limited to, *inter alia*, enlargement, extension of the powers of the Community, harmonisation of taxation, the Common Foreign and Security Policy and the Justice and Home Affairs Policy. Agreement by simple majority is reserved to procedural matters. It follows that by far the most common voting mechanism employed in Council meetings is qualified majority voting, and this applies to all acts adopted in the field of food law. Where provision is made for a qualified majority, the votes of the Member States are weighted in accordance with Article 205 EC as follows: Germany, France, United Kingdom and Italy have 10; Spain has 8; Belgium, Greece, Netherlands and Portugal have 5; Austria and Sweden have 4; Denmark, Finland and Ireland have 3; and Luxembourg has 2. A qualified majority is obtained when at least 62 of the total 87 votes support the decision; 26 of the votes (29%) constitute a qualified minority.

3.3 European Parliament ("the Parliament")

The European Parliament[6] represents, in the words of the 1957 Treaty of Rome, "the peoples of the States brought together in the European Community." The first direct elections to the European Parliament were held in June 1979. There are now 626 representatives ("MEPs" – Members of the European Parliament) elected for a period of 5 years. The president is elected by the MEPs in a secret ballot. The Treaties of Maastricht and Amsterdam have transformed the European Parliament from a consultative

---

[6] The Parliament's Web site address is: http://www.europarl.eu.int

assembly into a parliament with significant legislative and supervisory powers. It sits both in Brussels and in Strasbourg in France.

3.3.1   Legislative power

It is the Parliament's legislative power that will have most impact upon the development of EU food law. The Treaty of Amsterdam increased these powers by:

● amending the co-decision procedure to give the Parliament powers equal to those of the Council in this legislative process (see below); and

● by broadening the application of the co-decision procedure to the majority of harmonisation measures aimed at creating the internal market and also to areas where further democratic participation in the decision-making process was considered to be particularly needed (such as employment, social policy, public health, consumer protection and data protection).

3.3.1.1   Internal procedures

There are 17 standing committees whose remit covers every area of EU policy and which carry out the preparatory work for the plenary sessions of the Parliament. Of greatest relevance for food-related issues will be the Environment, Public Health and Consumer Policy Committee and the Legal Affairs Committee. The members and detailed activities of each committee are available from the Parliament's Web site.

The Parliament generally conducts its legislative duties as follows:

i)   The relevant parliamentary committee appoints a *rapporteur* from among its members to draft a report on the Commission proposal under consideration.

ii)   The Commission representative appears before the committee in order to clarify the Commission's approach and the stance it has adopted in the Council. (This gives the committee a useful insight into the activities of the Commission and an ability to monitor the Commission's work more effectively.)

iii) The *rapporteur* submits a draft report to the committee for discussion.

iv) After consideration, the draft report is put to the vote in the committee and possibly amended.

v) The report is then discussed in a plenary session of the Parliament (week-long plenary sessions are held every month), amended if necessary and put to the vote in plenary session.

Thus the Parliament adopts its position on a legislative proposal.

3.3.1.2   The co-decision procedure

Co-decision puts the Parliament as a legislature on an equal footing with the Council. It is a procedure that encourages the two institutions to reach agreement: if agreement is not reached the draft legislation in question has to be abandoned. It has become by far the most commonly used legislative procedure in the EU and signals the growing importance of the Parliament in shaping Community legislation[7].

i)   <u>First reading</u>

The starting point is a Commission proposal that is sent to the Council, the Parliament, and any committees to be consulted. The Parliament then takes its first reading and sends its opinion to the Council. The Economic and Social Committee and the Committee of the Regions are also given an opportunity to set out their position at this stage.

If the Parliament does not make any amendments to the Commission proposal, or the Council accepts all the amendments proposed by the Parliament, the proposal may be adopted at this stage of the procedure.

---

[7] The following paragraphs should be read in conjunction with the diagram in Appendix I to this book, which provides a graphic overview of the co-decision procedure and may be particularly useful for those seeking to lobby the institutions over the contents of draft proposals.

Otherwise, the Council, having considered the Parliament's opinion, adopts a common position by a qualified majority, which it then communicates to the Parliament, stating fully the reasons that led it to adopt its common position. The Commission informs the Parliament fully of its position as well. A second reading before Parliament is then required.

ii)   <u>Second reading</u>

The Parliament now has 3 months in which to do one of three things:

- If it approves the common position or has not taken a decision within 3 months, the legislative proposal is deemed to have been adopted in accordance with the Council's common position.

- If it rejects the common position outright (for which a majority of all members would be required), the legislative process is at an end; the Council no longer has the option of convening the Conciliation Committee.

- If it proposes amendments to the common position (for which a majority of all members would be required) the following procedure is invoked. The amended text is forwarded to the Council and the Commission which deliver further opinions.

The Council then has 3 months from receipt of the amended text from the Parliament within which to do one of two things:

- The Council first of all has the opportunity to adopt by qualified majority the common position as amended by Parliament, in which case all the proposed changes must be accepted; however, the Council must act unanimously on the amendments of the Parliament on which the Commission has delivered a negative opinion.

- But if the Council rejects certain amendments or the majority needed for their adoption cannot be obtained, then the President of the Council, acting in consultation with the President of the Parliament, must convene a Conciliation Committee within 6 weeks, consisting of 15 representatives from each institution to consider the Council's common position in the light of Parliament's proposed amendments. The aim is to achieve a workable compromise, which can be adopted by the required majorities in the Council and Parliament. The Commission also takes part in the Conciliation Committee's proceedings with a view to helping to achieve the necessary consensus.

iii)   Third reading

If the Conciliation Committee approves a joint text, the Council and Parliament must confirm its acceptance in a third reading within 6 weeks. Irrespective of the Commission's position regarding the draft compromise, a qualified majority in the Council is sufficient for its adoption (unless unanimity is required under the Treaties). Adoption by Parliament requires an absolute majority of the votes cast. The legislative proposal is then deemed to have been adopted as a legal instrument by Parliament and the Council.

If the joint draft is rejected at the third reading or the conciliation procedure fails, the proposal is deemed not to have been accepted. The legislative process is then at an end.

3.3.2   Supervisory powers

The Parliament has important supervisory powers. It has the power to reject the Commission's draft annual budget; the budget does not therefore come into effect until it has been signed and approved by the President of the European Parliament. It also exercises powers of supervision over all the activities of the Commission and the Council. It can set up committees of inquiry and can put written or oral questions to the Commission and the Council. It approves the nomination of the Commission President and appoints the College of Commissioners (all 20 members) by a vote of confidence. It also has the right to censure the Commission - a power that it threatened to invoke in 1999, causing the resignation of the Santer Commission.

3.4 European Court of Justice ("ECJ")[8]

The ECJ sits in Luxembourg and consists of 15 judges (one from each Member State) and 9 Advocates General. Its role is to ensure that Community law is interpreted and implemented in accordance with the Treaties, and in so doing it has the power to judicially review the actions of the Community institutions and the Member States. It has built up a significant body of case law in developing the general principles of Community law.

The ECJ is the highest judicial authority in matters of Community law; however, it is by no means the only judicial body empowered to apply Community law. The national courts of the Member States have primary jurisdiction over the administration of Community law for which their national authorities are responsible. In addition, many provisions of the Treaties and secondary legislation (regulations, directives and decisions) have direct effect, conferring rights on individuals that must be upheld in national courts. This is an important distinction to bear in mind. Whilst the ECJ is responsible for ensuring the uniform application of Community law, it is the national courts that must interpret and apply it on a daily basis. Although national courts can refer questions of interpretation to the ECJ for guidance, there is in fact no hierarchical relationship between the two, and the ECJ does not act as a final court of appeal from national courts.

3.4.1 Types of proceeding

3.4.1.1 Proceedings against Member States for failure to fulfil an obligation (Articles 226 and 227 EC)

Such proceedings enable the ECJ to determine whether a Member State has fulfilled its obligations under Community law. Actions may be brought by

---

[8] The ECJs Web site address is: http://curia.eu.int. Case law from June 1997 can be downloaded from this site.

the Commission or (less often) by another Member State. If the ECJ finds that an obligation has not been fulfilled – a typical example being that a directive has not been fully transposed – the Member State must comply with the Court's judgment or face a fixed or periodic penalty.

3.4.1.2   Judicial review – supervisory capacity of the ECJ (Articles 230, 231, 232 and 233 EC Treaty)

A Member State or Community institutions can challenge the legality of Community legislation if it infringes principles of Community law. The acts and omissions of Community institutions may be annulled on similar grounds. Individuals ("natural or legal persons") may in certain limited circumstances challenge the decisions of the Community institutions that are of individual concern to them and the ECJ may prescribe interim measures before finally declaring the act void if the challenge is well founded.

3.4.1.3   Actions for damages (Articles 235 and 288 EC Treaty)

In an action for damages based on non-contractual liability, the ECJ can rule on the liability of the Community for damage caused by its institutions or servants in the performance of their duties.

3.4.1.4   Appeals

The Court may hear appeals, on points of law only, against judgements of the Court of First Instance.

3.4.1.5   Preliminary rulings (Article 234 EC Treaty)

In domestic litigation involving the interpretation of Community law, the national courts, if unsure as to the interpretation or validity of a Community legal instrument, may[9] request the ECJ to give a preliminary ruling before making its final determination. The interpretation of the ECJ is binding on the

---

[9] By contrast, national courts of final appeal must request a preliminary ruling if unsure as to the interpretation and validity of a Community legal instrument.

referring court. Such a system of co-operation increases the prospects of Community law being applied uniformly within the EU. After the ECJ gives its ruling, the national court to which it is addressed must apply the law as interpreted by the ECJ. The preliminary ruling will also serve as clear guidance to all other national courts in the EU facing similar points of law.

3.5   Court of First Instance ("CFI")

The CFI was established in 1988 under the Single European Act to ease the mounting workload of the ECJ. The CFI is not a Community Institution *per se* but a constituent component of the ECJ. Nevertheless, it has its own registry and rules of procedure. Cases handled by the CFI are identified by a "T" (for tribunal), whilst those referred to the Court of Justice are prefaced with a "C" (for court).

Although the CFI was originally responsible for only a limited range of cases, a review of its responsibilities carried out in 1993 extended its jurisdiction to all direct actions for judicial review brought by individuals against Community acts, contractual disputes and actions brought by Community civil servants ("fonctionnaires") against the institutions (essentially staff disputes).

3.6   Treaty of Nice (enlargement)

Recent amendments to the EC Treaty were agreed by the Heads of State and Government in Nice in December 2000. The Treaty of Nice will incorporate a number of far-reaching changes into the EC Treaty, the overriding purpose of which is to reform and prepare the EU's institutional machinery for the task of enlargement. There are 13 applicant countries with which accession negotiations are open: Estonia, Lithuania, Latvia, Poland, Czech Republic, Slovakia, Hungary, Slovenia, Bulgaria, Romania, Malta, Cyprus and Turkey. Of those, Estonia, Poland, Hungary, Slovenia, Czech Republic and Cyprus have been the front-runners most likely to join before 2005.

3.6.1   Institutions

From 2005 the Commission will consist of one Commissioner from each Member State. The President of the Commission will be appointed by the Council under qualified majority voting and will be given enhanced powers.

The distribution of seats in the European Parliament will be amended (by reducing the number of seats allocated to existing Member States) to accommodate MEPs from the candidate countries.

The system of qualified majority voting in the Council will change in 2005, with a new system calculated to distribute the number of votes given to each Member State in accordance with their respective population size (including the 12 candidate countries).

The CFI will have jurisdiction for all actions for judicial review (i.e. no longer limited to natural or legal persons), all actions in tort, and may in specific circumstances be entitled to give preliminary rulings.

3.6.2   Legislative process

Qualified majority voting in the Council will be further extended to cover appointments within the Commission, industrial policy, cross-border judicial co-operation and the common commercial policy.

A major part of the visa, asylum and immigration policy will in future be adopted under the co-decision procedure.

3.6.3   Conclusions

The EU has indicated its hope that accession negotiations with the leading applicant countries will be concluded in time for the first new Members to take part in the European Parliament elections in June 2004. However, a referendum on the Nice Treaty in Ireland in May 2001 failed to ratify it – thereby presenting the EU with its first obstacle on the long road to enlargement.

4. FREE MOVEMENT OF GOODS IN THE INTERNAL MARKET

4.1 Establishment of the Internal Market

4.1.1 Introduction

The "Common Market" created by the Treaty of Rome in 1958 is based on the principle of free movement of goods in a customs union, a prerequisite for which is the elimination of tariff and non-tariff barriers between Member States. A signal lack of progress in the fulfilment of this key objective led to the establishment of the single market in the early nineties, also known as the internal market (as distinct from the Community's external market in trade with third countries). In 1985, the Commission produced a White Paper on the single market which identified 282 legislative measures necessary to establish an internal market and set a deadline of the end of 1992 by which they had to be implemented. The reforms heralded by the White Paper marked a political turning point in the Community's history; the Community has since evolved from a free trade area into being a single market of fully integrated economies with some 370 million consumers - the world's largest in terms of purchasing power. The near completion of the internal market by early 1993 was considered to be one of the great successes of the Commission under the leadership of Jacques Delors.

4.1.2 History

The internal market is underpinned by "four freedoms" enshrined in the EC Treaty, all of which are directly effective. Article 3.1.(c) EC provides that the internal market shall be: "characterised by the abolition, as between Member States, of obstacles to the free movement of goods, persons, services and capital." It is the free movement of goods that is a fundamental principle of EU food law.

The completion of a Community customs union in 1968 had effectively removed tariffs, levies and quotas from intra-Community trade; the prime purpose of the single market programme was therefore the need to remove non-tariff barriers. The reforms were specifically aimed at the removal of three types of non-tariff barrier:

i)   Physical frontiers were eliminated by abolishing border checks on people and goods.

ii) Technical frontiers created by national regulation of products and services were dismantled by means of harmonising directives and the development by the ECJ of the principle of mutual recognition.

iii) Tax frontiers were reduced by aligning national provisions on indirect taxation, VAT and excise duties.

The legislative burden of the internal market programme was ambitious and there was a concern felt in the Commission, with some justification, that the necessary momentum might be lost by the requirement for the Council to adopt all measures by unanimity. Accordingly, the 1986 Single European Act introduced qualified majority voting in the Council for internal market measures (for the limited exceptions see Article 95 EC), which succeeded in expediting their adoption. Since the enactment of the Maastricht Treaty, the co-decision procedure, in which the Council acts as a co-legislator with the Parliament, has been applied to internal market measures.

4.1.3   Success rate

By 1993, approximately 90% of the legislative measures foreseen by the 1985 White Paper had been adopted, including full liberalisation of capital movements and a total abolition of checks on goods at internal frontiers. Since 1993, the Commission has maintained the momentum towards completion of the internal market by issuing annual updates on its operation and action plans of legislative intent in the form of communications to the Council and Parliament. However, a pervasive obstacle to the completion of the internal market has been the failure by Member States to transpose, or correctly transpose, harmonising directives. In such circumstances, the Commission has not shied away from using its enforcement powers: since 1995 the number of default notices (the first stage in infringement proceedings under Article 226 EC) issued has consistently exceeded an annual figure of 200.

4.2   Free Movement of Goods

4.2.1   Treaty Articles[1]

Even before, and now in tandem with, the Commission's programme of harmonisation of the internal market, the ECJ has played an effective role in protecting and promoting the principle of free movement of goods within the Community. Articles 28, 29 and 30 EC are the relevant provisions. Article 28 provides:

"Quantitative restrictions on imports and all measures having equivalent effect shall be prohibited between Member States."

Article 29 provides:

"Quantitative restrictions on exports, and all measures having equivalent effect, shall be prohibited between Member States."

Limited derogations to the above prohibitions above are contained in Article 30 (see paragraph 4.2.6, p38). The interpretation of these provisions has led to a number of significant decisions in the ECJ.

4.2.2   Definitions of measures having equivalent effect to quantitative restrictions

Obstacles to the free movement of goods that arise from domestic rules laying down certain specifications, typically in the form of designation, size,

---

[1] In 1991, an Agreement on the European Economic Area ("EEA") between the Community and European Free Trade Area ("EFTA") applied from 1994 the EC Treaty provisions concerning free movement of goods, persons, services and capital to Iceland, Norway and Lichtenstein, the remaining members of EFTA other than Switzerland that did not ratify the Agreement. The supervision of the Agreement falls under the jurisdiction of an EFTA Court and the ECJ.

weight, composition, presentation labelling and packaging, constitute measures of equivalent effect prohibited by Article 28 EC. The Court has consistently held that Article 28 covers any measure imposed by a Member State that is capable, directly or indirectly, actually or potentially, of hindering intra-Community trade.[2] This is so even if the rules apply without distinction to both national and imported products unless their application is incapable of restricting imports or can be justified by a public interest objective under Article 30 taking precedence over the requirement for free movement of goods.

4.2.3   Mutual recognition

The principle of "mutual recognition" was first defined in 1979 in the celebrated *Cassis de Dijon* case,[3] a decision of the ECJ that, in part, spurred the Commission into launching its single market action programme in 1985.

Cassis de Dijon is a blackcurrant-based liqueur manufactured in France. The West German authorities sought to prohibit its import into the German market on the grounds that its alcoholic content was below the minimum of 25% by volume laid down by German law for liqueurs. The German Government had sought to justify the prohibition on the grounds that it restricted the proliferation of alcoholic beverages with low alcohol content because such beverages were more likely to induce a tolerance towards alcohol than more highly alcoholic beverages. The ECJ disagreed, holding that the legislation in question was not necessary on any public interest grounds but was discriminatory:

"14. It is clear from the foregoing that the requirements relating to the minimum alcoholic content of alcoholic beverages do not serve a purpose which is in the general interest and such as to take precedence over the requirement for free movement of goods, which constitutes one of the fundamental rules of the Community. [...]

---

[2] See *Procureur du Roi v Dassonville* (Case 8/74).
[3] *Rewe v Bundesmonopolverwaltung für Branntwein* (Case C-120/78)

It therefore appears that the unilateral requirement imposed by the rules of a Member State of a minimum alcoholic content for the purposes of the sale of alcoholic beverages constitutes an obstacle to trade which is incompatible with the provisions of Article 30 [now Article 28] of the Treaty.

There is therefore no valid reason why, provided that they have been lawfully produced and marketed in one of the Member States, alcoholic beverages should not be introduced into any other Member State; the sale of such products may not be subject to a legal prohibition on the marketing of beverages with an alcohol content lower than the limits set by the national rules."

The significance of the *Cassis de Dijon* decision cannot be overstated. Its purport is to allow a product that has been lawfully marketed in one Member State to be imported into another without restriction, unless a public interest ground or mandatory requirement can be successfully invoked. This principle, the principle of mutual recognition, is therefore of the greatest importance in ensuring the free movement of goods within the Community; this is especially so in areas that are still not subject to harmonised rules.

4.2.4   Examples of measures having equivalent effect

Applying the reasoning of the ECJ in *Cassis de Dijon*, the following have been held to be measures having equivalent effect to quantative restrictions.

i)   Requirements as to the composition of products. In *Commission v France* (Case C-184/96) the Commission applied to the ECJ for a declaration that a French regulation concerning the composition of preparations with *foie gras* as a base was incompatible with Article 28 EC. The regulation prescribed minimum *foie gras* content, maximum ingredient levels and presentation and packaging details, and further reserved the use of *foie gras* trade descriptions and sale of *foie gras*-based products only to products meeting these requirements. In response, the French Government argued, *inter alia*, that the requirements were necessary for the protection of the consumer, who was entitled to know the true nature of the product concerned, and also to prevent false trade descriptions from being permitted. The ECJ agreed with the first objective but considered that there were less restrictive ways of achieving it, such as labelling concerning the nature and characteristics of the product for sale (thus applying the principle of proportionality). With regard to protecting trade descriptions, the ECJ did not exclude the possibility that Member States might legitimately require alteration of the denomination of a foodstuff, but only where a product presented under a particular denomination was so different, as regards its composition or production, from the products generally known under that denomination in the Community that it could not be regarded as falling within the same category (see, to this effect, *Ministère Public v Deserbais* (Case C-178/84) and *Geffroy* (Case C-366/98)). However, the ECJ considered in the case of *foie gras* that the mere fact that a product did not wholly conform to the requirements laid down in national legislation on the composition of certain foodstuffs with a particular denomination did not mean that its marketing could be prohibited.[4]

ii)   Prohibitions on the use of generic terms. In *Guimont* (Case C-448/98) M. Guimont, the technical manager of a *laiterie* in France, was prosecuted for offering for sale foodstuff with deceptive labelling. He was in possession of 260 whole Emmenthal cheeses without rinds, in contravention of French legislation, which specified the characteristics of Emmenthal as being: "a firm cheese produced by curing, pressing and salting on the surface or in brine; of a colour between ivory and pale yellow, with holes of a size between a cherry and a walnut; *hard dry rind*, of a colour between golden yellow and light brown". In his

---

[4] For a recent exposition of the principle, in relation to a Belgian law prohibiting the marketing in its territory of bread and other bakery products whose salt content exceeds 2%, see the opinion of Advocate General Colomer in *Christina Bellamy v Procureur du Roi* (C-123/00), in which he concluded that such a law violated Article 28 EC.

defence, M. Guimont was able to prove that Emmenthal without rind was lawfully manufactured or marketed in other countries of the Community and that the *Codex Alimentarius* of the UN Food and Agriculture Organization (FAO) and the World Health Organization (WHO) referred to the consumption of Emmenthal without rind. The French court in Belley decided to refer the case to the ECJ for a preliminary ruling on the lawfulness of the prosecution. The ECJ held that:

● the mere fact that a national rule was not applied to imported products (as was the case here) in practice did not exclude the possibility of its having effects that could indirectly or potentially hinder intra-Community trade.

● in this case, the national rule in issue constituted a measure having equivalent effect to a quantitative restriction on imports within the meaning of Article 28 of the Treaty in so far as it applied to imported products. National legislation that subjected goods from other Member States, where they were lawfully manufactured and marketed, to certain conditions in order to be able to use the generic designation commonly used for that product was likely to make the marketing of that product more difficult and thus impede trade between Member States.[5]

● even if the difference in the maturing method between Emmenthal with rind and Emmenthal without rind were capable of constituting a factor likely to mislead consumers, it would be sufficient, whilst maintaining the designation of "Emmenthal", for the designation to accompanied by appropriate labelling highlighting that difference.

● the absence of rind could not therefore be regarded as a characteristic justifying refusal of the use of the Emmenthal designation for goods from other Member States where they were lawfully manufactured and marketed under that designation.

---

[5] See *Smanor* (Case 298/87)

iii) Declarations of nationality or origin. For the reasons given by the ECJ in the above two decisions, such requirements have been held to constitute measures having equivalent effect. (In *Procureur du Roi v Dassonville* (Case 8/74), a Belgian law requiring imported Scotch whisky to be accompanied by a certificate of origin was considered to be a quantitative restriction.)

iv) Restrictions on advertising that discriminate against imported products have consistently been held to offend against Article 28 EC (see *Verein Gegen Unweisen in Handle v Mars* (Case 470/93))

4.2.5   Selling arrangements

In contra-distinction to the above, the ECJ has held that certain selling measures may not infringe Article 28. In *Keck and Mithouard* (Case 267-8/91), criminal proceedings in a French court for reselling goods at a loss were referred to the ECJ. The Court distinguished *Cassis de Dijon* in the following way:

> "16. However, contrary to what has previously been decided, the application to products from other Member States of national provisions restricting or prohibiting certain selling arrangements is not such as to hinder directly or indirectly, actually or potentially, trade within Member States....*provided that those provisions apply to all affected traders operating within the national territory and provided that they affect in the same manner, in law and fact, the marketing of domestic products and of those from other Member States.*

> 17. Where those conditions are fulfilled, the application of such rules to the sale of products from other Member States is not by nature such as to prevent their access to the market or to impede access any more than it impedes the access of domestic products. Such rules therefore fall outside the scope of Article 30 [now Article 28] of the Treaty."

Rules relating to selling arrangements, as opposed to rules relating to goods themselves (e.g. composition, packaging, labelling), may not, therefore, fall within the ambit of Article 28, so long as the imported product enjoys equal access to the market of the importing Member State as national goods. The rationale for excluding selling arrangements from Article 28 is that, although they may affect the total volume of sales, they do not discriminate between imported and national goods. The following measures have accordingly been held not to have the equivalent effect of a quantitative restriction: a national ban on Sunday trading;[6] limiting the sale of processed milk for infants to pharmacies;[7] limiting the sale of tobacco to authorised tobacconists;[8] prohibitions on sales at a loss;[9] and the prohibition on advertising of products outside, for example, pharmacies.[10]

4.2.6   Article 30 derogations

Article 30 provides that:

"The provisions of Articles 28 and 29 shall not preclude prohibitions or restrictions on imports, exports or goods in transit justified on grounds of public morality, public policy or public security; the protection of health and life of humans, animals or plants; the protection of national treasures possessing artistic, historical or archeological value; or the protection of industrial and commercial property. Such prohibitions or restrictions shall not, however, constitute a means of arbitrary discrimination or a disguised restriction on trade between Member States."

---

[6] *Punto Case v PPV* (Case C- 69/93)

[7] *Commission v Greece* (Case C-391/92)

[8] *Banchero* (Case C-387/93)

[9] *Keck*

[10] *Hunermund v Landesapothekerkammer* (Case C 292/92)s

A restriction on imports that are lawfully marketed in other Member States will be permissible only in so far as it complies with the requirements of Article 30 EC. Each of its provisions has been strictly construed by the ECJ and made subject to a requirement of proportionality.[11] Furthermore, Article 30 will be invoked increasingly rarely as the approximation of standards in the production and marketing of food products through the adoption of directives continues: safeguard clauses in harmonising directives are generally treated as providing sufficient protection for Member States, thereby obviating the need for recourse to Article 30. For example, in *Moorman* (Case 190/87), the ECJ held that the existence of Community measures harmonising certain health inspections for poultry meant that a state could no longer resort to defences based on Article 30 in an attempt to justify national rules.

There follows below, however, an analysis of the ECJ's ruling in three cases concerning the scope in Article 30 of "the protection of health and life of humans" as a means of derogating from the principle of free movement of goods. Whilst these cases pre-date the recognition of public health as an official EU competency by the Maastricht Treaty, the reasoning of the Court gives a useful insight into the foundations on which the EU's consumer protection policy has been developed.

In *Officier van Justitie v Sandoz BV* (Case 174/82), Dutch authorities prohibited the sale of muesli bars that contained added vitamins. The bars were on sale in Germany and Belgium. It was accepted that vitamins could be beneficial to health, but it was also acknowledged that excessive consumption of vitamins could be harmful to health. Scientific evidence was not, however, certain as regards the point at which consumption of vitamins became excessive and there were no detailed Community harmonisation measures in place regulating vitamin additives. The ECJ held, in supporting the action of the Dutch authorities, that, in so far as there are uncertainties in the state of scientific research, it is for the Member States, in

---

[11] Proportionality is a general principle of EC law which requires the legislative means employed to be no more than the strict minimum required to achieve a particular end (see also chapter 2).

the absence of harmonisation, to decide what degree of protection of the health and life of humans they intend to assure, having regard to the free movement of goods in the Community. This will, however, be subject to the principle of proportionality. Therefore, any such measures will need to be restricted to what is necessary to attain the legitimate aim of protecting public health.

By contrast, in *Commission v Germany* (Case 178/84 – "the German Beer case"), a German law that banned the marketing of beer containing non-natural additives on public health grounds was held not to fall within Article 30. In so finding, the ECJ referred to the expert reports of the Community's own scientific committees and the *Codex Alimentarius* Committee of the FAO and the WHO, both of which indicated that the additives were not only harmless but also served a legitimate technological purpose.

In an example of the ECJ's application of the principle of proportionality in the context of Article 30, the Court held in *Commission v UK* (Case C-124/81) that the UK's requirement for imported UHT milk to be subject to an import licence was disproportionate. A certificate from the authorities of the exporting Member States would have sufficed to assure the UK authorities of the origin of the imported milk.

4.3   Conclusions

The Community institutions have adopted, and the Member States transposed, over 300 harmonising measures as part of the single market programme, and those that relate to the regulation of food are considered in later chapters. In consequence, cases of indirect barriers to the free movement of intra-Community trade in foodstuffs will be fewer and further between. More prevalent in the current climate of food safety concerns will be direct barriers to trade raised on the grounds of the protection of public health. But in areas that are as yet unregulated by harmonised rules, national legislation that restricts the free circulation of goods within the Community will be compatible with the Treaty only if it is applied without distinction to national products and imported products or only in so far as it is necessary to satisfy overriding public interest requirements under Article 30, and is proportionate to the objective pursued.

Since the BSE crisis in the UK, the dioxin scandal in Belgium, and public reaction within the Community to the marketing of genetically modified organisms, the food regulation in the EU has turned from assuring the free movement of foods to focus on food safety, one of the top priorities for the current Commission, and one which is considered in the next chapter.

5. KEY DEVELOPMENTS IN EU FOOD SAFETY POLICY

5.1 Introduction

In 1992 the Maastricht Treaty made public health an official EU competence for the first time, though subject to subsidiarity, and in 1999 the Amsterdam Treaty recognised consumer protection as a policy in its own right to a much greater extent than before. Article 153 EC, introduced by the Amsterdam Treaty, now constitutes a legal basis for a diverse range of actions in this field at Community level. It provides:

> "In order to promote the interests of consumers and to ensure a high level of consumer protection, the Community shall contribute to protecting the health, safety and economic interests of consumers, as well as promoting their right to information, education, and to organise themselves in order to safeguard their interests."

It is worth noting that Article 153 raises certain consumer entitlements to a *right* under EU law. Commissioner Byrne has described Article 153 as a "quasi-constitutional obligation".

Food safety came to the public's attention when, in March 1996, the British Government published research results pointing to a possible link between BSE (bovine spongiform encephalopathy) in cattle and new-variant Creutzfeldt-Jakob disease in humans[1]. This caused a deep crisis of confidence in the safety of the food being offered to European consumers and led to a total ban on UK exports of live cattle and cattle products. And then, in the wake of BSE, came the Belgian dioxin crisis, concerns over US hormone-implanted beef, and the foot-and-mouth epidemic. It is not entirely surprising then that promoting food safety in a climate of low

---

[1] It is now assumed that new-variant Creutzfeldt-Jakob disease is caused by the transmission of BSE to humans. Since its first diagnosis in 1996, there have been 99 confirmed or suspected cases in the EU. All bar four (three in France and one in Ireland) have occurred in the UK. (Figures taken from D.G. Sanco's Web site). See paragraph 5.4.5, p.68.

consumer confidence has become one the Commission's strategic objectives. In its communication "Strategic Objectives 2000-2005 – Shaping a New Europe" (9 February 2000) the Commission comments that people "... rightly insist that food safety standards should be higher. They are worried by the impact of new technologies and new ways of doing business in an increasingly frontier-free Europe. They expect their rights to be bolstered. The Commission intends to take forward the proposals in its White Paper on Food Safety and on the Creation of a European Food Authority".

Implementing the White Paper on Food Safety (COM (1999) 719) is the key task for David Byrne, former Attorney-General of Ireland and current Commissioner of the newly formed Health and Consumer Protection DG (DG SANCO). As an expression of policy intent, the White Paper introduces the most far-reaching reforms in the area of food regulation and consumer protection since the creation of the European Economic Community in 1957. In the Commission's own words, it "makes proposals that will transform EU food policy into a proactive, dynamic, coherent and comprehensive instrument to ensure a high level of human health and consumer protection" (Chapter 2). And, in conclusion (Chapter 9), it states: "Greater transparency at all levels of Food Safety policy is the golden thread throughout the whole of the White Paper and it will contribute fundamentally to enhancing consumer confidence in EU food safety policy." In all, 84 new initiatives for improving the quality and safety of food production are proposed by the White Paper.

To fully understand the direction in which food safety policy is heading within the EU, operators should be aware of the essential policies and strategies contained within the White Paper.

5.2 White Paper on Food Safety – Synopsis of Major Changes[2]

5.2.1 Chapter 1: Introduction

● The Commission indicates that it will implement the legislative actions outlined in the White Paper in accordance with the timetable for the Action Plan, which is set out in the Annex to the Paper (and at Appendix 1 of this book).

● The White Paper represents the changes that the Commission proposes in the area of food legislation following the publication of the Green Paper (COM (97) 176 final), which it supersedes. It seeks to establish an integrated food policy for the EU "from farm to table".

5.2.2 Chapter 2: Principles of food safety

● Feed manufacturers, farmers and food operators (i.e. all stakeholders in the food chain) will have the primary responsibility for food safety; national authorities will monitor and enforce this responsibility through the operation of national surveillance and control systems; and the Commission will concentrate on evaluating the ability of national authorities to deliver these systems through audits and inspections.

● Feed, food and their ingredients must be traceable; adequate procedures to facilitate traceability must be introduced by stakeholders.

● The formulation of food policy should be transparent, involving all stakeholders in the food chain and allowing them to make effective contributions to new developments.

● Risk analysis must be the foundation on which food policy is based. Risk analysis has three components: risk assessment (scientific advice and information analysis); risk management (regulation and control); and risk communication. Where appropriate, the precautionary principle[3] will be applied to risk management evaluations.

---

[2] The following excerpts outline the major reforms. For further analysis, the White Paper can be downloaded from D.G. Sanco's Web site.
[3] See paragraph 5.4.4, p.65

5.2.3 Chapter 3: Essential elements of food safety policy: information gathering and analysis – scientific advice

- Reinforced systems are required to respond to the overall objective of improving consumer health protection and restoring confidence in the EU's food safety policy. More particularly:

  - Monitoring and surveillance: the integration of both data collection systems and analysis of data will become the two guiding principles employed to draw maximum benefits from the current systems of data gathering. The expertise of the Commission Joint Research Centre will be increasingly used in this regard.

  - Early warning systems: the scope of the Rapid Alert System for Food will be extended to all food and feed, not simply for foodstuffs intended for the final consumer.

  - Research: the present system must be endowed with sufficient flexibility and financial resources to be able to finance R&D projects in direct response to food emergencies.

  - Scientific co-operation: a priority for the work programme of the scientific committees will be to coordinate information compiled by national institutions in order to build a European picture of risk assessment.

  - Obligatory consultation of the scientific committees: much food safety legislation already requires the Commission to consult a scientific committee prior to making proposals that may affect public health. In future, all food safety legislation will have to be adequately based on independent scientific advice.

  - Scientific committees: the increased demands placed on the committees have led to a mounting backlog of work and also to an inability to respond quickly to food scares (the dioxin crisis in Belgium being a prime example). Scientific networks between Member States should undertake much of the time-consuming preparatory work of these committees.

- It is intended that many of these concerns will be addressed by the creation of a European Food Authority.

5.2.4   Chapter 4: Towards establishing a European Food Authority

- The Commission believes that major structural changes are necessary in the way in which food safety issues are handled, having regard to its experience of crisis management over the last few years. The principal change required is to separate the functions of risk assessment and risk management. The establishment of a new food authority is considered by the Commission to be the most effective means of achieving this and thereby increasing public health protection and restoring consumer confidence.

- The primary responsibilities of the Authority will be risk assessment and risk communication on food safety issues. Risk management (formulating legislation and overseeing a system of effective control) will remain distinct from the Authority and within the competence of the Commission.

Independence

- The Authority will have a separate legal personality from the EU Institutions in order to enhance its independence and impartiality.

Risk assessment

- The scope of the Authority should be to provide scientific advice and information to the Commission on all matters having a direct impact on consumer health and safety arising from the consumption of food. It will oversee primary food production, industrial processes, storage, distribution and retailing. Its remit will cover both risk and nutritional issues, and will take into consideration risk assessments in the environmental and chemical sectors where these overlap with risk assessment in relation to food.

- The scientific work currently undertaken by the Scientific Committees relating to food safety will become a core part of the Authority's mandate.

- The Authority will have its own budget for the commissioning of *ad hoc* immediate research in response to unforeseen health emergencies and will liaise with the Commission's Joint Research Centre, national scientific agencies and international organisations.

- The Authority will need to harness and co-ordinate the scientific information available within the Community and worldwide. To do so, it will need to work closely with national scientific agencies in charge of food safety to create a network of scientific contacts in the Community and worldwide with the Authority at its centre. If properly exploited, the sharing of information should not only facilitate earlier identification of potential health scares but also lighten the workload of the Scientific Committees, which will be able to concentrate more fully on their core task of preparing opinions.

- The Authority will operate within the Rapid Alert System and will play the key role in the EU's response to a food scare.

Communication of risk

- The communication of risk is key to ensuring that consumers are kept informed and to reducing the spread of unfounded food safety scares. It will require scientific opinions and the results of surveillance and monitoring programmes to be made widely and rapidly available to the public, subject to the usual requirements of commercial confidentiality.

- The Authority should become the automatic first port of call when scientific information on food safety and nutritional issues is sought or food safety concerns have been identified. Again, it will also need to ensure that appropriate information on these issues is published.

- However, the Commission will remain responsible for the communication of risk management decisions that it takes.

5.2.5   Chapter 5: Regulatory aspects

● The Green Paper on the general principles of food law foresaw a need for a major review of food legislation. The White Paper further reflects the need to create a coherent and transparent set of rules governing food law, and places food safety as the primary objective of future legislation. The full range of measures proposed – and estimated timetable for implementation – is presented in the "Action Plan on Food Safety"[4]. The proposals are as extensive as they are diverse. The following are considered to be priority measures[5].

- ● a proposal for a General Food Law Directive, which will embody the principles of food safety as set out in Chapter 2 of the White Paper;

- ● a proposal for a Regulation on official food and feed safety controls;

- ● a proposal for a Regulation on feed and novel feed;

- ● a proposal for amending Regulation 258/97 on novel foods and novel food ingredients;

- ● a proposal for a Regulation on hygiene;

- ● proposals for amending Directives 89/107/EEC and 95/2/EC on food additives;

- ● a Regulation on the labelling of GMO-free foodstuffs;

- ● a proposal for amending Directive 79/112/EEC on the labelling, presentation and advertising of foodstuffs;

5.2.6   Chapter 6: Controls

● Food control legislation over the last 30 years has been carried out on a piecemeal basis. The consequence is a lack of uniformity. In addition, recent food safety crises have highlighted deficiencies in some national

---

[4] See Appendix I

[5] All of which are discussed further in this chapter or under further chapter headings

systems of control. The Commission considers that there is therefore a clear need for a Community framework of national control systems, the operation of which would remain a national responsibility. The framework will have three core elements:

i) operational criteria adopted at Community level, which national authorities would be expected to meet; these criteria would form the key reference points against which the competent authorities would be audited by the Food and Veterinary Office (FVO), allowing a consistent approach to the audit of national systems to develop.

ii) the development of Community control guidelines; these would promote coherent national strategies and identify risk-based priorities and the most effective control procedures.

iii) enhanced administrative co-operation in the development and operation of control systems within the Community. This envisages an increased exchange of information between national authorities, more comprehensive training of national officials, and longer-term strategic thinking at Community level.

● The importance of having effective and harmonised health controls at the external borders of the European Union has become very clear; but the legal basis for border checks needs to cover non-animal products as well as animal products, and to identify a more effective Community-level control system.

5.2.7   Chapter 7: Consumer information

Risk communication

● Transparency in all areas of food safety policy is a key element to developing consumer confidence. Since 1997, the Commission has implemented a new approach to transparency by making available to the public information on scientific advice and on inspection and controls. The Commission recognises the consumer as a stakeholder in the food chain who is fully entitled to consultation on all aspects of food safety. Further disclosure and more discussions between scientific experts and consumers in public forums can be expected.

Labelling and advertising

● Within the World Trade Organisation (WTO), the Commission will pursue multilateral guidelines on labelling.

● The Commission intends to propose a new amendment to the Labelling Directive, which will preclude the current possibility for components of compound agreements that form less than 25% of the final product not to be indicated.

● The Commission continues to consider that labelling and advertising of foodstuffs should not contain health claims relating to the prevention, treatment or cure of human disease (as prohibited by the current Labelling Directive). However, the Commission will consider whether specific provisions should be introduced to govern "functional" claims and "nutritional" claims, and also whether the Misleading Advertising Directive should be extended to cover such claims.

● The Commission will further consider the opportunity to revise or introduce specific labelling provisions for certain categories of foods, such as novel foods.

Nutrition

● The Commission considers that there is a growing need to inform consumers about the nutritional contents of the food they consume.

   ● In respect of dietetic foods, the Commission will elaborate a specific Directive on foods intended to meet the needs resulting from intense muscular effort.

   ● It will also prepare a report on foods intended for diabetes sufferers and on the pre-conditions for defining food as "low-sodium", "sodium-free" and "gluten-free".

- The Commission will submit to the Council and to Parliament two proposals for Directives on food supplements (concentrated sources of nutrients such as vitamins and minerals) and fortified foods (foods to which nutrients have been added).

- The Commission is considering the development of a comprehensive nutritional policy and will present an action plan for this purpose in due course.

5.2.8   Chapter 8: International dimension

- The key factor applied to imported foodstuffs and animal feed is that they must meet health requirements that are at least equivalent to those set by the Community for its own production.

- The Commission plays an active role within the WTO, where it represents the Member States, to ensure that the rights of Member States to maintain high public health standards for food safety are both respected and protected internationally. To this end, the Commission will seek to agree a methodology for the use and scope of the precautionary principle in the area of food safety with the other members of the WTO.

- The accession of the EU to the *Codex Alimentarius* and the International Office of Epizootics will be a priority.

- As regards the future enlargement of the Community, it is essential that the candidate countries have implemented food safety legislation and control systems equivalent to those already in use within the Community before they join.

5.3   Regulation 178/2002/EC (the General Food Law Regulation) – the Cornerstone White Paper Reform

On 28 January 2002, the Council of Ministers and Parliament adopted Regulation 178/2002 "laying down the principles and requirements of food law, establishing the European Food Safety Authority and laying down procedures in matters of food safety." This is the cornerstone of the

Commission's legislative reforms following the publication of the White Paper.

It provides a legal framework for food safety, laying down the legitimate objectives and definitions of food law, with the primary aim being to ensure that unsafe food and feed is not placed on the European market. Food is defined as "any substance or product, whether processed, partially processed or unprocessed, intended to be, or reasonably expected to be, ingested by humans. Food includes drink, chewing gum and any substance, including water, intentionally incorporated into food during its manufacture, preparation or treatment." "Food" does not include feed, live animals unless they are prepared for human consumption, plants prior to harvesting, medicinal products (within the meaning of Directives 65/65/EEC and 92/73/EEC), cosmetics, tobacco, narcotics, residues and contaminants. Feed is defined as "any substance or product, including additives, whether processed or unprocessed, intended to be used for oral feeding to animals." Food and feed is deemed to be unsafe if it is injurious to human health or unfit for human consumption.

Chapter II ("General Food Law") of the Regulation outlines the Community's commitment to ensuring that food production shall be based on high-quality, transparent, independent scientific advice; it provides an overarching requirement for only safe, traceable food to be placed on the market and ensures the rights of individuals to be informed and to have access to safe foods; it incorporates the precautionary principle and it creates the European Food Safety Agency[6]. Existing food law principles and procedures should be adopted by Member States as soon as possible and by 1 January 2007 at the latest to comply with the Regulation.

---

[6] The proposed name of the "European Food Authority" was subject to a last-minute amendment in the Council of Ministers. In that same meeting, disputes between Sweden, Finland and Italy over the location of the Authority led to an impasse, with Silvio Berlusconi famously arguing Italy's cause on the grounds that it was the birth place of *Parma* ham; at present, the Authority will be temporarily based in Brussels.

5.3.1 Food/feed business operators[7]

The Regulation outlines the responsibilities of food and feed business operators as follows:

> "Food business" is defined as "any undertaking, whether for profit or not and whether public or private, carrying out any of the activities related to any stage of production, processing and distribution of food". "Feed business" is defined as "any undertaking whether for profit or not and whether public or private, carrying out any operation of production, manufacture, processing, storage, transport or distribution of feed including any producer producing, processing or storing feed for feeding to animals on his own holding".

Food and feed business operators at all stages of production, processing and distribution within the business under their control are required by Article 17 to ensure that foods or feeds satisfy the requirements of food law that are relevant to their activities and to verify that such requirements are met. The Regulation sets in stone, therefore, that it is the food business operators who bear the primary responsibility for compliance with food law. The test to be applied is a stringent one.

If a food business operator considers or has reason to believe that a food that it has imported, produced, processed, manufactured or distributed is not in compliance with the food safety requirements, it must immediately initiate procedures to withdraw the food in question from the market and inform the national food authority. Where the product has reached the consumer, the operator shall inform the consumer of the reasons for withdrawal and, if necessary, recall products already supplied to them. The food business operator is further required to assist other operators and the national food authority in question in the process of tracing food. Operators will be expected to be able to identify, and have readily available to the

---

[7] See Articles 17, 19 and 20

competent authorities on demand, any person from whom they have been supplied with food, feed, a food-producing animal, or any substance intended to be, or expected to be, incorporated into a food or feed[8]. And, if a food business operator considers or has reason to believe that it has placed food on the market that is injurious to human health, it shall immediately inform and cooperate with the competent authority concerned. The above provisions apply equally to feed business operators.

The burden on the food business operator is clearly intended to be a formidable one. A suspicion of non-compliance with food safety requirements, rather than fear of injury to human health itself, is sufficient to require the withdrawal of the food from the relevant market.

5.3.2   European Food Safety Agency (EFSA)

At the time of going to press, the EFSA is in the process of being established in accordance with the legal base provided for in the Regulation. Its functions will be as follows[9]:

- The independent scientific evaluation of risks on behalf of the Commission, the Parliament and Member States.

- To promote and coordinate the development of uniform risk assessment methodologies.

- The collection, analysis and communication of scientific data.

- Safety evaluations of dossiers put forward by industry for EU level approval of substances or processes.

- To establish a system of networks of organisations operating within its field of competence.

- To identify emerging risks.

---

[8] See Article 18
[9] See Article 23

- To ensure that the public and interested parties receive rapid, reliable, objective and comprehensible information on issues coming within its responsibility

- To be included in the Rapid Alert System, which will remain, as it is now, managed by the Commission.

Risk assessment within the EFSA will be undertaken by a Scientific Committee and permanent Scientific Panels, each with its own sphere of competence.

The Scientific Committee will be responsible for the general coordination necessary to ensure consistency within the scientific opinion procedure, in particular with regard to the adoption of working procedures and harmonisation of working methods of the Panels. It shall also provide opinions on multisectoral issues falling within the competence of more than one Scientific Panel, and on issues that do not fall within the competence of any of the Panels.

The following Scientific Panels will be established:

- A Panel on food additives, flavourings, processing aids and materials in contact with food.

- A Panel on additives and products or substances used in animal feed.

- A Panel on plant health, plant protection products and their residues.

- A Panel on genetically modified organisms.

- A Panel on dietetic products, nutrition and allergies.

- A Panel on biological hazards.

- A Panel on contaminants in the food chain.

- A Panel on animal health and welfare.

The above Committee and Panels will replace much of the EU's current system of scientific committees[10] from the date of appointment of their members[11]. Until then, the current system of scientific committees remains in place.

5.4   Further Aspects of Food Safety Policy

5.4.1   *Veterinary and phytosanitary inspections and the scientific committees*

As a result of the BSE crisis, the Commission decided to reform its safety protection and food hygiene responsibilities by separating the departments responsible for drawing up legislation, scientific consultation and inspection and by improving the transparency and dissemination of information[12]. The principal reforms, announced by President Santer in his address to the European Parliament in February 1997, were:

- The transformation of the Community Office for Veterinary and Phytosanitary Inspection and Control, attached to the DG Agriculture, into a Food and Veterinary Office attached now to DG SANCO.

- The creation of eight committees to replace the scientific committees dealing with consumer health protection, and a Scientific Steering Committee (SSC), concerned mainly with the multi-disciplinary aspects of BSE[13] and co-ordination of the working procedures of the other eight committees.

---

[10] See further below at paragraph 5.4.12
[11] See Article 62
[12] See Commission Communication COM(97) 183 fin. of 30 April 1997, and the EU Web site at http://europa.eu.int/scadplus/leg/en
[13] See Commission Decision 97/404/EC and 97/579/EC, and the EU Web site at http://europa.eu.int/scadplus/leg/en

5.4.1.1   The Food and Veterinary Office (FVO)

The FVO is responsible for monitoring Member States' and third countries' compliance with Community veterinary, phytosanitary and food hygiene legislation. To this end, the FVO performs audits and on-the-spot inspections to check whether food safety regulations are being observed along the entire production chain, in Member States themselves, in candidate countries seeking to join the EU, or in countries that export to the EU. It then reports its findings and recommendations to national and Community authorities, and makes them available to the general public[14].

The inspections and audits it carries out relate to:

- Foodstuffs of animal origin, for which it examines monitoring systems in the Member States, the use of chemicals (veterinary medicinal products, growth stimulants, pesticides) and imported products;

- Foodstuffs of vegetable origin, in particular pesticide residues on fruit and vegetables and organic fruit and vegetables, including imported products;

- Animal health and notable epidemics (e.g. classical swine fever, BSE);

- Animal welfare and zootechnics (e.g. transport, slaughtering);

- Plant health (monitoring of organisms harmful to plants, genetically modified organisms, pesticides)[15].

5.4.1.2   Scientific committees[16]

Scientific advice guiding the development of EU food law is principally obtained from the work of the eight scientific committees and the Scientific

---

[14] Its inspection reports are published on the Commission Web site at www.europa.eu.int/comm/food/fs/inspections/vi/reports/index.

[15] As set out by the Commission at http://europa.eu.int/scadplus/leg/en

[16] Full details of the committees, their members and publications can be obtained from the DG SANCO (*www.europa.eu.int/comm/food*) Web site.

Steering Committee. Consultation with scientific committees may be mandatory or discretionary, depending on the legal instrument concerned[17]. The three guiding principles that are intended apply to the work of the scientific committees are: the excellence of their members, their independence, and the transparency of their advice. High-quality advice is – needless to say – of the utmost importance to the Commission in the formulation of policy.

Decision 97/404/EC sets up a Scientific Steering Committee responsible for assisting the Commission in obtaining and coordinating scientific opinions relating to consumer health and food safety (it carries out the functions that the Scientific Committee of the EFSA will in future assume). The SSC:

- Delivers scientific advice on matters that are not covered by the mandates of the specialised scientific committees;

- Delivers advice on the multidisciplinary aspects of transmissible spongiform encephalopathies (TSEs);

- Assists the Commission with the identification of those areas where compulsory consultation of the scientific committees could be appropriate;

- Arranges for the review of new risk assessment procedures, particularly in regard to foodborne diseases and the transmissibility of animal diseases to man;

- Draws the attention of the Commission to any specific consumer health problem[18].

---

[17] It will be seen from later chapters that consultation with a scientific (and regulatory) committee is often a mandatory part of the authorisation for marketing of a foodstuff. The relevant Scientific Committee in the case of marketing of a foodstuff is the Scientific Committee for Food.

[18] As set out by the Commission at http://europa.eu.int/scadplus/leg/en. The SSC has delivered significant opinions on the following subjects: BSE in general, specified risk materials, BSE risk in geographical areas, the UK Date Based Export Scheme and BSE in sheep. See further at paragraph 5.4.5.

Decision 97/579/EC establishes eight scientific committees: the Scientific Committee on Food; the Scientific Committee on Animal Nutrition; the Scientific Committee on Animal Health and Welfare; the Scientific Committee on Veterinary Measures relating to Public Health; the Scientific Committee on Plants; the Scientific Committee on Cosmetic Products and Non-food Products intended for Consumers; the Scientific Committee on Medicinal Products and Medical Devices; and the Scientific Committee on Toxicity, Ecotoxicity and the Environment.

These scientific committees are consulted where required by Community legislation and on other questions of particular relevance to consumer health and food safety. They are responsible for:

- Examining risk assessments by scientists belonging to national organisations;

- Developing new risk assessment procedures in areas such as food-borne diseases and the transmissibility of animal diseases to man;

- Drafting scientific opinions designed to enable the Commission to evaluate the scientific basis for recommendations, standards and guidelines prepared in international forums;

- Evaluating the scientific principles on which Community health standards are based[19].

All committees adopt their own rules of procedure, which are publicised. Their agenda, minutes and opinions are also available to the public, subject to the need for commercial confidentiality.

The mandate of the Scientific Committee for Food (SCF) (of most relevance to this work) is as follows:

"Scientific and technical questions concerning consumer health and food safety associated with the consumption of food products and in particular questions relating to toxicology and hygiene in

---

[19] As set out by the Commission at http://europa.en.int/scadplus/leg/en

the entire food production chain, nutrition, and applications of agrifood technologies, as well as those relating to materials coming into contact with foodstuffs."[20]

In practice, the work carried out by the SCF is dominated by questions and opinions arising from the obligatory requirement in foodstuff legislation to consult the SCF in relation to proposals for health-related measures[21].

When established, the Scientific Committee and Panels of the EFSA will replace the Scientific Committee on Food, the Scientific Committee on Animal Nutrition, the Scientific Veterinary Committee, the Scientific Committee on Pesticides, the Scientific Committee on Plants and the Scientific Steering Committee.

5.4.1.3   Regulatory committees

Measures on which the scientific committees have delivered an opinion are formally adopted by the Commission in regulatory committees, whose function is to authorise the implementation of recommendations and proposals. The most important in terms of food legislation is the Standing Committee on Foodstuffs[22]. Regulatory committees are composed of national experts from Member States and chaired by a Commission official. If the Committee rejects a proposal or fails to deliver an Opinion, the matter is then referred to the Council of Ministers. The Council may reject the proposal by simple majority within 3 months.

---

[20] See http://www.europa.eu.int/comm/food/fs/sc

[21] In 1998, the SCF delivered opinions on over 80 substances to be used in the production of food packaging and several food additives (see http://europa.eu.int/comm/food/fs/sc).

[22] When the EFSA is fully established the name of this committee will change to the Standing Committee on the Food Chain and Animal Health.

5.4.2   Official controls[23]

Official control of foodstuffs at Member State level is regulated by Council Directive 89/397/EEC on the official control of foodstuffs[24]. This Directive lays down general principles governing the official inspection of foodstuffs, food additives, vitamins, mineral salts, trace elements and materials coming into contact with foodstuffs to ensure that they comply with provisions designed to prevent risks to public health, to ensure fair trading and to protect consumer interests. It also sets out procedures for carrying out inspections both on a regular basis and in those instances when non-compliance is suspected. Items subject to inspection include raw materials, semi-finished products, finished products, and cleaning and maintenance products used in connection with the production of foodstuffs.

The Directive further prescribes the nature and role of food inspectors, training standards, and quality standards for laboratories involved in inspection and sampling. Member States are obliged to draw up forward programmes laying down the nature and frequency of inspections and must inform the Commission annually of their implementation. On the basis of this information, the Commission draws up recommendations for coordinated inspection programmes within the Community. The following recommendations for coordinated inspection programmes have been made, highlighting areas of particular concern to food safety:

- Recommendation 92/540/EEC concerning adulteration of orange juice, nitrates, nitrites, and nitrites in infant formulas containing vegetables, checking the weight of deep-frozen seafood, and microbiological analysis of ice cream and of prepared dishes.

- Recommendation 94/175/EC concerning aflatoxin B1 in products that might contain it (in particular food products for children),

---

[23] See also Chapter 6 on food hygiene

[24] The Directive is supplemented by Directive 93/99/EEC, which provides for the Commission to monitor the national control systems. An inspection body was created and attached to DG SANCO for this purpose.

Listeria in meat-based pâtés for sale, fraud relating to deep-frozen fish based products, and fraud relating to goats' and ewes' cheese.

- Recommendation 95/77/EC concerning adulteration of soluble coffee, microbiological checks on refrigerated salads and seasoned crudités, claims on honey, and the temperature of quick-frozen foodstuffs sold in the retail sector.

- Recommendation 96/290/EC concerning microbiological assessment of dried and fermented ready-to-eat meat and meat products, migration of plasticisers into foods, temperature of chilled foods on display for sale, and benzo(a)pyrene in smoked pork products.

- Recommendation 97/777/EC concerning aflatoxins in spices and contamination of food products for persons suffering from a food allergy or hypersensitivity.

- Recommendation 98/133/EC concerning aflatoxins in ground nuts and pistachios.

- Recommendation 99/26/EC concerning ochratoxin A in coffee and additives in foodstuffs[25].

The system of official controls of foodstuffs is, however, about to be overhauled. In the Commission's view, the current system as it is applied is fragmented and incoherent and fails to distinguish effectively between the roles of the Commission and the Member States. And the level of control in some Member States is considered to be especially poor. The Commission is therefore drafting a proposal on official controls, in line with the White Paper, which aims:

- "To create a clear Community framework for control systems, in which the respective responsibilities of Member States and the Commission are clearly set out; and

---

[25] As set out by the Commission at http://europa.eu.int/leg/eu//rb

● To implement a harmonised, coordinated and effective system of control on imports of food and feed."

In relation to national control systems, whilst it notes that the first responsibility for ensuring quality control rests with the food business operator – a legal requirement now enshrined in the General Food Law Regulation – the Commission is proposing a harmonised Community-wide approach to the design and development of national control systems. This will involve establishing operational criteria for national food control authorities, qualification and training requirements for their staff, and the implementation of documented control procedures. As part of this approach, Member States will be obliged to develop national control plans[26]. In effect, much of the responsibility for official controls will in future fall upon the Member States.

The Commission intends to oversee the role of the national competent authorities by carrying out audits of national control plans and conducting inspections of particular sectors of control points.

The importance of this proposal should not be underestimated. Commissioner Byrne has described the reform of food control legislation as "the third pillar" of the Community's food safety policy, the first being an effective range of food safety legislation and the second being the European Food Safety Authority. A published proposal can therefore be expected shortly.

5.4.3   Contaminants in foodstuffs[27]

Contaminants in foodstuffs are regulated by Council Regulation 315/93/EEC on procedures for contaminants in food. A contaminant is "any substance not intentionally added to food which is present in such food as a result of the production (including operations carried out in crop husbandry, animal husbandry and veterinary medicine), manufacture, processing, preparation,

---

[26] Speech by Denis Byrne at the 9th East West Agricultural Forum - Green Week, Berlin, 10-12 Jan 2002
[27] I am grateful to the material provided by DG Sanco on its Web site in preparing this section

treatment, packing, packaging, transport or holding of such food, or as a result of environmental contamination."[28] Extraneous matter, such as insect fragments and animal hair, are not covered by this definition. Contaminants may enter into food at any stage of production and can obviously be harmful to human health. It is therefore essential that contaminants are kept at levels that are toxicologically acceptable. Food contamination can be reduced through good working practices. Good working practices include measures such as preventing food contamination at source, for example by reducing environmental pollution and applying appropriate practices and technologies in food production, handling, storage, transport, processing and packaging[29].

The basic principles of Community legislation concerning contaminants are set out in the Regulation, which provides that:

- Food containing a contaminant in an amount that is unacceptable from the public health viewpoint and in particular at a toxicological level shall not be placed on the market;
- Contaminants shall be as low as can be reasonably achieved following good practices;
- Maximum tolerances shall be established for certain contaminants and contained in a non-exhaustive Community list;
- Where maximum tolerances have not been set at Community level, national provisions may apply[30].

Maximum levels at Community level have been set only for nitrates in spinach (fresh, preserved, deep-frozen) and fresh lettuce (protected and open-grown) and aflatoxin B1 and aflatoxin total in groundnuts, nuts, dried fruit and cereals and aflatoxin M1 in milk[31]. Sampling methods and methods

---

[28] Article 1 Regulation 315/93/EEC

[29] As set out by the Commission at http://europa.eu.int/comm/food/fs/sjp/fcr

[30] As set out by the Commission at http://europa.eu.int/comm/food/fs/sjp/fcr

[31] Regulation 194/97/EC

of analysis for aflatoxins have also been laid down in legislation[32]. In its White Paper, the Commission announced that it intended to set maximum levels for further contaminants including dioxins, ochratoxin A, cadmium, 3-MCPD, lead, Fusarum toxins, organotin compounds and PAHs.

5.4.4   Risk Management Commission Communication on the precautionary principle[33]

Towards the end of the last decade, the Council and Commission became increasingly concerned that "the precautionary principle", not being defined in the EC Treaty or any other EU instrument at that time, was being developed and applied unsystematically in different policy areas within the EU and internationally. In a bid to define (and limit) the scope and applicability of the principle in a range of policy areas, the Commission, on 2 February 2000, published a Communication on the precautionary principle.

What is meant by the precautionary principle? Put simply, it is applied where an unacceptable risk to human health has been identified but further scientific information, data or research is needed to arrive at a complete assessment of the risk. In other words, where scientific evaluation does not allow a risk to be determined with sufficient certainty, the precautionary principle may be invoked. The principle should be considered within the structured approach to the analysis of risk (which, besides risk evaluation, includes risk management and risk communication), and most particularly in the context of risk management (decision making). The Commission considers that judging what is an acceptable level of risk for society is an "eminently political responsibility"[34], and its general policy has been to seek a high level of consumer protection within the EU. However, it stresses that the principle should not be confused with the element of caution that scientists typically apply in their assessment of scientific data.

---

[32] Directive 98/53/EC
[33] Address by David Byrne to the Economist Conference on Precautionary Principle, Paris, 9 November 2000.
[34] COM(2000)1, which can be downloaded

The guidelines further state that the precautionary principle should be informed by three specific principles:

- Implementation of the principle should be based on the fullest possible scientific evaluation. As far as possible, this evaluation should determine the degree of scientific uncertainty at each stage;

- Any decision to act or not to act pursuant to the principle must be preceded by a risk evaluation and an evaluation of the potential consequences of inaction;

- Once the results of the scientific evaluation and/or the risk evaluation are available, they should be publicised to all interested parties.

Besides these specific principles, the general principles of good risk management remain applicable when the precautionary principle is applied. They are as follows:[35]

- Proportionality: tailoring measures to the chosen level of protection. A total ban will not be a proportional response to a potential risk in every case and the principle is not to be seen as a justification for achieving zero risk.

- Non-discrimination in the application of measures: comparable situations should not be treated differently.

- Consistency: measures should be of a comparable scope and nature to those already taken in equivalent areas where all scientific data is available.

- Examining costs and benefits. This entails comparing the overall costs to the Community of action and lack of action, in both the short and the long term. This is not simply an economic cost-

---

[35] See paragraph 6.3 of the communication

benefit analysis: its scope is much broader, and includes non-economic considerations, such as the efficacy of possible options and their acceptability to the public. (In the conduct of such an examination, account should be taken of the general principle and the case law of the ECJ to the effect that the protection of health takes precedence over economic considerations).

● Review of the measures in light of scientific progress. Measures based on the precautionary principle should be maintained only for so long as scientific information is incomplete or inconclusive, and the risk is considered too high to be imposed on society, in view of the chosen level of protection.

In its past application, the precautionary principle has invariably attracted contention, often being perceived as disguised protectionism by those seeking to sell foods and foodstuffs within the EU, and risk managers applying the principle walk a fine line between restricting the freedom and rights of individuals or corporations to trade and reducing the risk of adverse effects on the environment and human health. The Communication is therefore an attempt to define where the correct balance lies and to suggest effective guidelines for the principle's consistent application[36].

The principle is now enshrined in Article 7(1) of the General Food Law Regulation, which provides:

> "In specific circumstances where, following an assessment of available information, the possibility of harmful effects on health is identified but scientific uncertainty persists, provisional risk management measures necessary to ensure the high level of health protection chosen in the Community may be adopted, pending further scientific information for a more comprehensive risk assessment."

---

[36] For a discussion of the scope of the precautionary principle in the context of international trade in food, see chapter 12.

Food business operators should therefore expect to see the principle informing more EU risk management decisions.

5.4.5   The Community's response to the BSE crisis

Bovine spongiform encephalopathy (BSE) is a disease of the brain in cattle. It was first diagnosed in the UK in 1986 and spread rapidly in the 1990s when meat and bone meal from cattle carcasses were used in cattle feed. Variant Creutzfeld-Jakob Disease (VCJD) is generally presumed to be caused by the transmission of BSE to humans. As at February 2001, the number of recorded cases in the UK was 180,903, and, in the remainder of the EU, 1,924[37].

The incidence of BSE in the EU is still of considerable concern[38]. The Community has put in place the following measures to combat its transmission to food for human consumption:

- A ban on the feeding of mammalian meat and bone meal (MBM) to cattle, sheep and goats, as of July 1994.

- Higher processing standards for the treatment of animal waste (133 °C, 3 bars of pressure for 20 min) to reduce infectivity to a minimum, as of 1 April 1997.

- Surveillance measures for the detection, control and eradication of BSE, as of 1 May 1998.

- The requirement to remove specified risk materials (SRMs) such as spinal cord, brain, eyes, tonsils, part of the intestines from cattle, sheep and goats throughout the EU from 1 October 2000 from the human and animal food chains. The obligation is also mandatory for imports of meat and meat products from third world countries into the EU except Argentina, Australia, Botswana, Brazil, Chile, Namibia, Nicaragua, Norway, New

---

[37] "Frequently Asked Questions about BSE", 6 April 2001 (http://europa.eu.int/comm/food/fs/dsc)

[38] More thorough and pervasive inspection for BSE has led to an increase in its detection in other Member States.

Zealand, Paraguay, Singapore, Swaziland and Uruguay since 1 April 2001.

● The introduction of targeted testing for BSE, with a focus on high-risk animal categories, from 1 January 2001.

● The prohibition from using dead animals not destined for human consumption in feed production from 1 March 2001 onwards[39].

Following more recent scientific advice, and continuing consumer concern, the Commission has adopted a series of additional measures:

● The testing for BSE of all cattle aged over 30 months destined for human consumption; their carcasses may not be released before a negative test result has been obtained. (Austria, Finland and Sweden may derogate from the requirement to test healthy cattle pursuant to a scientific assessment showing that BSE risk in those Member States is lower.)

● The extension of the list of SRMs to include the entire intestine and vertebral column of bovines. (SRMs are removed at slaughter from all cattle aged over 12 months and destroyed.)

● A ban on the use of mechanically recovered meat derived from bones of cattle, sheep and goats in feed and food.

● A proposal to tighten up treatment standards for ruminant fats is expected[40].

● A Regulation concerning the prevention and eradication of Transmissible Spongiform Encephalopathies (TSE)[41].

---

[39] As set out by the Commission at http://europa.eu.int/comm/food/fs/tse
[40] See paragraph 5.4.11
[41] 999/2001/EC

The Commission's FVO carries out inspections to verify the correct implementation and enforcement of these measures by the competent national authorities.

In addition to the measures outlined above, a number of other important Commission proposals originating from the BSE crisis are currently under examination for adoption by the Council of Ministers and the European Parliament:

- A major concern in the Commission is the continued uncertainty over the true incidence of scrapie in sheep; scrapie is thought to mask the presence of BSE. The Commission has recently adopted a decision to increase substantially the level of testing of sheep over 18 months for TSEs. The number of tests will increase more than threefold to approximately 560,000 a year.

- A proposal for a Regulation on Animal By-products, which will ensure that only material from animals fit for human consumption can be used in animal feed.

5.4.6   Zoonoses

Zoonosis is the scientific term for any disease or infection that is likely to be naturally transmitted from animals to man, and a zoonotic agent is any bacterium, virus or parasite that is likely to cause a zoonosis. The most commonly known zoonosis is salmonella. The alarming rise of salmonella poisoning in humans, occasionally with fatal consequences[42,] led to the adoption in 1992 of the Zoonoses Directive (92/117/EEC). This Directive[43] sought i) to control and reduce the incidence of salmonellosis in poultry breeding and laying flocks; ii) to establish a reporting system for the occurrence of all zoonoses in the human population, in domestic animals,

---

[42] See paragraph 5.4.11

[43] According to the findings of the EU's Scientific Committee on Veterinary and Plant Health, in approximately 5% of salmonella cases sequellae (similar to reactive arthritis) arise and in 2% of those cases (i.e. 1 in every 1,000 cases of salmonella) the patient dies.

in animal feeding stuffs, and in wildlife in order to assess priorities for future preventive action; and iii) to develop control measures for zoonoses other than salmonella.

Further, the Commission was required by the Directive to report to the Council on additional measures to be introduced to combat zoonoses. The recently published Report[44] comments, favourably, that increased activity by Member States in this field (as required by the Directive) has led to growing awareness of the threat posed to the consumer by zoonoses and that, despite the difficulty and expense of implementing the control regimes, the incidence of salmonella has stabilised or even decreased in Member States. However, the Report concludes that the number of human infections caused by "traditional" pathogens remains high and that "new" pathogenic, such as Campylobacter verotoxigenic *E. coli* (VTEC), pose an emerging but significant threat to human health[45]: "the figures have to be interpreted carefully, since it is likely that many human infections go unrecorded, with either patients failing to present to health services or no laboratory diagnosis being made, or the diagnosis not being reported centrally. The cases reported may in fact only represent the severe end of the spectrum of the disease. Despite this underreporting, it appears that the magnitude of these human health problems is significant."

As a result of these findings, the Commission has recently announced two Proposals for a Directive and a Regulation to implement a Community-wide strategy on the prevention and control of zoonoses[46]. Together with experts from the Member States, the Commission has identified seven common goals:

---

[44] As amended by Directives 97/22/EC and 1999/72/EC

[45] COM(2001) 451 final: "Report to the European Parliament and to the Council on the Measures to be put in force for the control and prevention of zoonoses."

[46] The figures reported by Member States for 1999 are as follows. Two zoonoses caused the major part of the reported cases of human illness: *Salmonella* (165,659 cases) and *Campylobacter* (126,981). Of the others, there were 8,309 cases of *Yersinia*, 3,843 of *Brucella*, 1,892 of verotoxigenic *E. coli*, 665 of *Listeria*, 554 of Echinococcus 309 for Toxoplasma, 155 for *Mycbacterium bovis* and 48 for Trichinella. No cases of human rabies were reported.

- "to create a system of monitoring of zoonoses based on harmonised rules, when necessary;

- to develop measures according to (the) "farm to table" principle, by producing safe food from healthy animals;

- to take account of the level of prevalence of zoonotic agents in the Member States;

- to give guarantees for the improvement of the safety of consumers by introducing pathogen reduction programmes to be implemented by the Member States;

- to give the flexibility needed for the Member States to achieve common targets; and

- to take account of concerns with regard to the spreading of zoonotic agents through animal trade."

In practice, what this implies is an intensified, multi-disciplinary approach to the reduction of all zoonoses with concomitant increased costs to national food authorities and food business operators. One of the main objectives of the Proposals is described as being "to ensure that any contamination or re-contamination carried by live animals or hatching eggs transferred from one holding to another can be eliminated[47], and the Commission recognises that public financing may be justified to bear some of the expense of achieving this. For food business operators, control measures will need to be put in place, or reinforced, throughout the food chain: in animal waste and feed processing, at farm level, in processing and distribution of foodstuffs of animal origin and at consumer level. Member States will have to implement programmes to reach pathogen reduction

---

[47] COM(2001) 451 final: "Proposal for a Directive on the monitoring of zoonoses and zoonotic agents, amending Council Decision 90/424/EEC and repealing Council Directive 92/117/EEC; Proposal for a Regulation on the control of salmonella and other foodborne zoonotic agents and amending Council Directive 64/432/EEC, 72/462/EEC and 90/539/EC." There follows a synopsis of the two proposals; further details can be found by downloading the Proposals from the *europa* Web site. (For details of how to use the Web site, see the Preface to this work.)

targets. Further co-ordination of monitoring and reporting systems will all be required. At Community level, through the auspices of the European Food Safety Authority informed by expert opinion from Member States, a scientific base for controlling pathogens will have to be established, supported by thorough risk assessment.

The proposals will also affect intra-Community and international trade: "The basic element in the proposal is to ensure that the purchaser of live animals or hatching eggs knows the status of the holding of origin of the animals. Nationally this can be achieved through national control programmes. However, concerning intra-Community trade, there is a need to use a health certification system[48]. Existing health certificates will therefore be amended by Commission Decisions to incorporate common criteria concerning zoonoses control. Further, only table eggs originating from flocks that have been tested negative for *Salmonella* Enteritidis and *Salmonella* Typhimurium will be allowed on the EU market. Similarly for poultry meat, a criterion of "absence of Salmonella in 25 g" will be applied.

Equivalent measures and a system of certification will also be required, for imports of relevant animals and eggs from third countries. Internationally agreed standards on the control of zoonoses do not, however, exist. The Agreement on the Application of Sanitary and Phytosanitary Measures (the "SPS Agreement"), with which members of the World Trade Organisation have agreed to comply, will therefore play a significant role in determining the validity of any measures taken by the Community to restrict the import of animals and eggs on the grounds of the risk to human health caused by zoonotic agents[49].

5.5   Conclusion[50]

A high level of consumer protection is the guiding principle that now defines the future development of EU food law. Over the next decade or so,

---

[48] Paragraph D3.3 of the Report
[49] Paragraph 2E of the Explanatory Memorandum
[50] The SPS Agreement is considered more fully in chapter 12

operators throughout the food chain should expect the regulation of food production to increase and change considerably in accordance with the Action Plan set out in the White Paper, and the heaviest burden of that change will be borne by food business operators themselves[51].

---

[51] Further aspects of food safety are dealt with in the following chapters. Suffice to say here that irradiation of food, which is not considered further in this work, is regulated under EU legislation by Directives 1999/2/EC and 1999/3/EC.

# 6.	FOOD HYGIENE

## 6.1	Introduction

Any consideration of Community regulation of food hygiene should be prefaced by the fact that the law on food hygiene is in the process of being entirely recast. There are 14 Directives concerning food hygiene that have been adopted since 1964 in response to the needs of the internal market. Their co-existence has led, over the years, to duplication and inconsistency, and consequently difficulty in interpretation and implementation. The Commission's plans for reforming and consolidating this area of food law were signalled in the White Paper and have been further developed in a series of Commission proposals[1]. Readers should be aware that these reforms envisage the repeal of all pre-existing Directives on food hygiene. The proposals are considered in greater detail later in this chapter. They are not expected to come into force until 1 January 2004.

It is not within the scope of this work to summarise the hygiene provisions of each of the "product-specific" Directives; this chapter will instead focus on the Directive of greatest general relevance, Council Directive 93/43/EEC on the hygiene of foodstuffs ("the general food hygiene Directive"), which lays down the general rules and procedures of verification that apply to food hygiene in the EU. Listed below in chronological order are the "product-specific" Directives that comprise the detailed food hygiene rules of the EU for various products[2]: Directive 64/433/EEC (fresh meat); Directive 71/118/EEC (poultry meat); Directive 77/99/EEC (meat products); Directive 91/492/EEC (milking hygiene); Directive 89/43/EEC (egg products); Directive 91/492/EEC (live bivalve molluscs (clams, mussels)); Directive 91/493/EEC (fishery products); Directive 91/495/EEC (rabbit meat and farmed game meat); Directive 92/45/EEC (game meat); Directive 92/46/EEC (milk and milk products);

---

[1] COM (2000) 438(1)-(5)

[2] The contents of these Directives can be downloaded from *Eur-Lex* on the *Europa* Web site at http://europa.en.int/eur-lex.

Directive 92/48/EEC (fishing vessels); Directive 92/118/EEC (gelatin, frogs legs and snails); and Directive 94/65/EC (minced meat).

6.2 Council Directive 93/43/EEC of 14 June 1993 on the Hygiene of Foodstuffs – the General Food Hygiene Directive

A lack of food hygiene in the preparation of food poses one of the most obvious and serious risks to human health. This Directive, which states in its recital that "Protection of human health is of paramount concern", lays down general rules of hygiene of foodstuffs and the procedures for verification of compliance with these rules. The observance of these rules by food business operators in the Member States is enforceable by national food authorities. The Directive does not apply to primary production; nor does it apply to foodstuffs in so far as they are regulated by the product-specific Directives listed above. However, the majority of the product-specific Directives do not extend to sales to the final consumer and so most retail and catering activities will be covered by this Directive. It was intended that the Commission should review the relationship of the specific food hygiene Directives with this Directive within 3 years of its adoption – but this review never took place.

Food hygiene means "all measures necessary to ensure the safety and wholesomeness of foodstuffs". The general rules of hygiene for foodstuffs are to be observed at all stages after primary production (e.g. harvesting, slaughter and milking). This includes food preparation, processing, manufacturing, packaging, storing, transportation, distribution, handling and/or offering for sale or supply of foodstuffs. "Wholesomeness" is defined as "food which is fit for human consumption as far as hygiene is concerned."

6.2.1 Obligations on food business operators

The food business operator (meaning any undertaking carrying out any of the processes cited above) is responsible for the hygiene conditions of the following operations: the preparation, processing, manufacturing, packaging, storing, transporting, distribution, handling and offering for sale or supply of foods. One of the most significant provisions of the Directive requires food business operators to identify the steps necessary to ensure food safety in their businesses in accordance with the principles of Hazard Analysis and Critical Control Points (HACCP). The implementation of hazard analysis and control principles requires the following:

- analysing the potential food hazards in a food business operation;
- identifying the points in those operations where food hazards may occur;
- deciding which of those points identified are critical to food safety – the "critical" points;
- identifying and implementing effective control and monitoring procedures at those critical points; and
- reviewing the analysis of food hazards, the critical control points and the control and monitoring procedures periodically and whenever the food business operations change.

In formulating the above, food business operators and national food authorities are additionally encouraged by the Directive to develop guides to good hygiene practice that can be implemented on a voluntary basis. These should have regard to the General Principles of Food Hygiene of the *Codex Alimentarius.*

However, microbiological criteria and temperature control measures for certain classes of foods should only be adopted in accordance with scientifically accepted principles, and to that end have to be approved by the Scientific Committee for Food before being employed by food business operators.

The Annex to the Directive lists extensive and detailed hygiene requirements with which the food business operator is obliged to comply. They fall under the following chapter headings[3]:

---

[3] Reiteration of the manifold requirements listed in the Annex to the Directive is not possible here; but see footnote 2.

Chapter I: general requirements for food premises (other than those specified in Chapter III)
Chapter II: specific requirements in rooms where foodstuffs are prepared, treated or processed
Chapter III: requirements for movable and/or temporary premises (e.g. marquees, market stalls, and mobile sales vehicles)
Chapter IV: transport of food
Chapter V: equipment requirements
Chapter VI: food waste
Chapter VII: water supply
Chapter VIII: personal hygiene
Chapter IX: provisions applicable to foodstuffs
Chapter X: training food business operators

6.2.2   National food authorities

National food authorities ("competent authorities") are responsible for ensuring that the standards of food hygiene practiced by food business operators are, at the very minimum, in accordance with the requirements of this Directive. (National food authorities are also entitled to introduce more stringent national hygiene requirements with the approval of the Commission so long as they do not act as barriers to trade.) The principal means of enforcement is through Directive 89/397/EEC on the official control of foodstuffs[4], which prescribes the inspection of foodstuffs by competent authorities. The food hygiene Directive further specifies that food hygiene inspections should include "a general assessment of the potential food safety hazards associated with the business. Competent authorities shall pay particular attention to critical control points identified by food businesses to assess whether the necessary monitoring and verification controls are being operated.[5]"

---

[4] See further in Chapter 5
[5] See Article 8

If such inspections, which often take place unannounced, establish a failure to comply with the HACCP guidelines, or the obligations set out in the Annex, national food authorities are empowered by the Directive to seize and destroy the foodstuff in question, and, if appropriate, temporarily close down the food business concerned. Such teeth are considered necessary to enforce food hygiene regulations.

6.2.3   Safeguard measures

If a hygiene problem likely to pose a serious risk to human health arises or spreads in the territory of a third country, the Commission, of its own volition or at the request of a Member State, and if time permits in consultation with the Member States, should:

- suspend imports from all or part of the third country concerned and if necessary the transit country; and/or
- lay down special conditions for foodstuffs from all or part of the third country concerned.

If, however, the Commission does not invoke the above safeguard measures at the request of a Member State, the Member State concerned may take interim protective measures to restrict the import of the foodstuff in question. The interim measures taken will then be subject to scrutiny by the Standing Committee on Foodstuffs for its approval, amendment or abrogation[6].

6.3   Proposals for Reform[7]

Two of the four proposed Regulations reform the law of food hygiene; the first reforms the official controls on products of animal origin, and the second reforms animal health rules[8].

---

[6] These measures are typical of the safeguard clauses found in EC food safety legislation
[7] None of which will be in force before 1 January 2004
[8] See footnote 1. The remaining two proposals for Regulations are considered at paragraphs 6.3.3 and 6.3.4 below.

In recasting existing legislation, the Commission's intention is to adopt a comprehensive and integrated approach to food hygiene, covering the entire production chain of foods of both animal and plant origin. At the heart of these reforms, and consistent with the spirit of the White Paper, is the achievement of a higher level of consumer protection from foodborne infections, and the tenet that underpins them is the principle that the food operator, whether farmer or grocer, bears full responsibility for the food produced and sold.

6.3.1 Proposal for a Regulation on the hygiene of foodstuffs[9]

In the period of consultation on this proposal, there was general agreement among Member States that the product-specific hygiene Directives should be consolidated and, further, that the replacement for the general food hygiene Directive 93/43/EEC should form the basis for hygiene measures applicable to all foodstuffs. As a consequence, the recasting of Directive 93/43/EEC in the form of this proposal will apply to products of animal origin as well. There are seven principal areas of reform.

i)   The HACCP system

In order to bring Community legislation into line with the more recently formulated principles of food hygiene laid down by the *Codex Alimentarius*, it is proposed that HACCP be introduced as a mandatory requirement for all food business operators (i.e. including those concerned with products of animal origin) other than those at the level of primary production. In addition, all operators will have to keep more detailed records of the own-check programmes they carry out so that national food authorities can monitor them more effectively.

---

[9] See the Explanatory Memorandum for further detail, from which this outline is taken (Web site: europa.en.int/comm/food/fs).

ii)   Food Safety Objectives ("FSO")[10]

The Commission wishes to focus more on the objectives that must be met to ensure food safety rather than prescribing detailed measures necessary to ensure food safety. That implies that food operators will have to conceive their own procedures for achieving a defined objective. The advantages of such a system are, in the Commission's view, simpler legislation, which can be limited to the setting of objectives, and more flexibility for food operators, who should establish documented systems on the means developed by them to meet the objectives set by law. Rather than fixing FSOs at this stage, which will in any event have to be based on sound scientific advice, the proposal lays down a procedure that will allow the Commission to fix FSOs in the future.

iii)   The tracing of food and food ingredients

Recent food emergencies have demonstrated that rapid identification of the origin of food and food ingredients is vital to ensure consumer protection. This proposal introduces such measures, again adding to the burden placed on the food operator, designed to facilitate tracing in cases of emergency:

- Food businesses will have to be registered by the competent national authority and allocated a registration number. The registration number of the food operator introducing the product into the food chain after primary production will follow the product to its destination. In certain cases where the competent authority seeks assurances about compliance of food businesses with hygiene rules prior to starting up such businesses, its approval of the food business will be required, in which event the approval number, rather than the registration number, will follow the product.

- Food businesses will be obliged to ensure that adequate procedures are in place to withdraw food from the market in cases of emergency, and

---

[10] An example of the principle of subsidiarity in operation. See further below at 6.3.1.vii

to keep adequate records, which must enable them to identify the supplier of any ingredients used in their operations.

The proposal also contains procedures for laying down more detailed rules on traceability.

iv) *Imports of products into the Community*

Provision is made in the proposal for foodstuffs imported into the Community to comply with Community hygiene standards[11].

v) *Exports of Community products to non-Member countries*

The proposal states that food exported to non-Member countries should not present a risk to human health. Such products must therefore meet at least the standards that apply for marketing within the Community, in addition to standards imposed by the non-Member country concerned[12].

vi) *The farm to table approach and primary production*

A significant reform introduced by this proposal is that the general food hygiene Directive should cover the entire food chain, rather than, as at present, only after primary production. Significantly, hygiene at farm level will therefore be regulated by this Directive for the first time. The Commission does not, at this stage, foresee requiring the HACCP system to be applied to primary production as it is to the rest of the food chain; in its place it recommends methods of control to be addressed in guides to good practice. One of those is the Good Animal Husbandry Practices (GAHP), compliance with which is ensured by the competent authorities.

---

[11] It is a requirement of the General Food Law Regulation (178/2002/EC), Article 11, that all food and feed imported into the Community for sale shall comply, at the least, with pre-conditions imposed by the Community.

[12] This again is a requirement of the General Food Law Regulation (Article 12)

vii)   *Flexibility*

The proposal reflects the principle of subsidiarity to the extent that it accepts that flexibility is needed for small businesses, especially those that are geographically remote, and for the manufacture of traditional products. It also accepts that the competent authorities of the Member States are in the best position to ensure the appropriate level of hygiene in these businesses without compromising the objectives of food safety.

6.3.2   *Proposal for a Regulation laying down specific hygiene rules for food of animal origin*

The Commission's intention is to consolidate the "patchwork" of product-specific Directives concerning food of animal origin into one Regulation containing a set of rules common to all foods of animal origin. Nonetheless, the Proposal is considered to be too complex to be applied uniformly to retail sale; hygiene in the retail sale of foods of animal origin will accordingly be left to the draftsmen of the Proposal for a general hygiene Regulation. There are seven principal areas of regulation and reform in the Proposal for specific hygiene rules for food and animal origin.

i)   *Product definition*

The definitions of products of animal origin contained in the present Directives have not been drafted or interpreted uniformly. Particular problems have been encountered by food operations that result in composite products. Some product-specific Directives will cover all the activities of a business that produce foodstuffs comprising different ingredients; but other businesses can be regulated by two or more separate Directives, depending on the products in question. To meet this flaw, the Commission has proposed that products of animal origin be categorised as follows:

- unprocessed (raw) products, such as meat, raw milk, eggs, fish and molluscs; and

- processed products such as meat products, egg products, and processed fish.

These two categories would then constitute the basis for defining the scope of the specific hygiene legislation for products of animal origin. The Commission further suggests in its Explanatory Memorandum that the hygiene of composite products could be satisfactorily covered by the general food hygiene Directive, it being understood that, in such products, the ingredient of animal origin is obtained in accordance with the specific hygiene rules contained in the annexes to this Proposal.

ii)   *Approval of establishments*
Manufacturing and processing plants of food of animal origin will continue to have to be approved by national competent authorities, and only those that are approved will be allowed to place their products on the market. Such establishments will receive an approval number, which will follow the products during marketing.

iii)   *Health marking*
The system of health marking for products of animal origin will remain, but the Commission recognises that it serves a less obvious purpose in the light of the systematic registration of food businesses and the existence of an identification number system that traces the product produced by each food business. Further debate will therefore be required on the future of health marks.

iv)   *Detailed requirements*
One of the main criticisms of the specific food hygiene legislation in force is that it is too prescriptive, leaving insufficient flexibility for new techniques to be developed. The Proposal reduces the level of detail in regulation in the following areas:

- areas of repetition
- through the introduction of the HACCP procedures to all foods; and
- through the introduction of codes of good hygiene practice.

However, it is recognised that sufficient detail is nonetheless necessary to ensure that correct procedures are implemented by food operators. The Commission will therefore monitor the effectiveness of the good practice guidelines implemented in Member States before deciding whether to replace detailed regulation with further guidelines once these Proposals are adopted. In certain cases, however, existing rules have been tightened in order to address recent outbreaks of foodborne diseases. New rules to prevent carcass contamination have been introduced, such as the need to present clean animals for slaughter, and the obligation to apply evisceration techniques that avoid the spilling of the gut contents on the carcass.

v)   Microbiological criteria
The Commission is currently reviewing the existing microbiological criteria to ascertain whether they should be updated. They will in due course be submitted for re-examination by the scientific committees.

vi)   Small production units
The present Proposal contains special rules for the infrastructure of small production units in the belief that they can produce safe products under fewer and specific rules adapted to their particular type of production.

vii)   Imports from non-Member countries
The Proposal applies standard tests for regulating imports from non-Member countries of products of animal origin destined for human consumption:

- audits and/or assessment of the past performance of the non-Member country competent authority and on-the-spot inspections to verify compliance/equivalence with EU standards. These are carried out by the Food and Veterinary Office;

- establishment of a list of non-Member countries matching EU standards;

- establishment of import conditions and certification requirements for each non-Member country; and

- establishment of a list of establishments in non-Member countries meeting EU standards.

6.3.3   Proposal for a Regulation for the organisation of official controls on products of animal origin intended for human consumption

Animal health rules are designed to prevent the spread of animal diseases such as swine fever and foot-and-mouth disease through products of animal origin. These rules are contained in the following Directives: Directive 72/461/EEC (fresh meat), Directive 80/215/EEC (meat products), Directive 91/67/EEC (aquatic animal products), Directive 91/494/EEC (poultry meat), Directive 91/495/EEC (rabbit meat and farmed game meat), Directive 92/45/EEC (game meat), Directive 92/46/EEC (milk and milk products). These will be recast into a single Regulation prescribing the means of eliminating animal hazards that can occur in products of animal origin.

6.3.4   Proposal for a Regulation laying down animal health rules governing the production, placing on the market and importation of products of animal origin intended for human consumption

Requirements for official controls are in force for different sectors, such as veterinary public health, animal health, foodstuffs and animal feed. This sectoral approach has led to inconsistency, duplication and loopholes in the relevant legislation. The Commission's proposal will therefore cover all aspects related to the official controls for the safety of both feed and foodstuffs, and the responsibilities of the competent authorities.

6.4   Conclusion

The EU regulation of the hygiene of foodstuff is piecemeal and complex, and in need of reform, principally through consolidation and clarification. Whilst the Commission recognises this, it is also concerned that hygiene rules should be reinforced to ensure that they meet their primary purpose of assuring the protection of human health. Although these proposals signal more intensive regulation in areas where the risk of contamination from unhygienic conditions is considered to be greatest, and stake great importance in the more effective scrutinising functions of the competent authorities, the greatest responsibility for the safety of the food we eat is placed on food operators throughout the food chain. The development of good practice guidelines and self-checking procedures is an important evolution in the regulation of food safety; but, needless to say, it will also add greatly to the administrative burden under which food operators will have to operate in the future.

7. FOOD LABELLING

7.1 Introduction

The primary purpose of EU rules on the labelling of foodstuffs is the need to inform and protect the consumer. Food production has become increasingly sophisticated, with the consequence that there is a growing demand among consumers to be better informed about the contents of the food they eat. This concern is reflected in Chapter 7 ("Consumer Information") of the White Paper, which sets out the Commission's proposals concerning the labelling of foodstuffs.

There are three main areas of labelling regulation of which the food producer should be aware:

i)   the Labelling Directive (2000/13/EC);

ii)   the recent Commission proposal (06.09.2001 COM (2001) 433 Final) to amend the Labelling Directive; and

iii) the Nutrition Labelling Directive (90/496/EEC).

7.2 The Labelling Directive

The first Labelling Directive (Council Directive 79/112/EEC of 18 December 1978 "on the approximation of the laws of the Member States relating to the labelling, presentation and advertising of foodstuffs") had been so frequently and significantly amended since its adoption that a consolidating Directive has recently been adopted ("the Labelling Directive"), which repeals the former Labelling Directive and its subsequent amendments and incorporates them into one single text: European Parliament and Council Directive 2000/13/EC.

Under this Directive, labelling is defined as meaning: "any words, particulars, trade marks, brand name, pictorial matter or symbol relating to a foodstuff and placed on any packaging, document, notice, label, ring or collar accompanying or referring to such foodstuff."

The purpose of the Directive is threefold: to maintain the smooth functioning of the internal market by ensuring that national labelling provisions for foodstuffs do not impede the free circulation of goods or create unfair competition; to prescribe a list of all the information that is in principle required on the labelling of all foodstuffs in the internal market; and thereby to safeguard consumers' interests by allowing them to make a choice in the full knowledge of the relevant components of their purchase.

The Directive contains the well-known provisions that labelling, presentation and advertising of foods should not mislead the consumer as to the characteristics of the food; nor should they attribute to the product effects or properties it does not possess; nor should they suggest that the food possesses special characteristics when in fact all similar products possess such characteristics. The European Court of Justice has consistently held that, in deciding whether consumers have been misled, national courts may take into account the "presumed expectations of an average consumer who is reasonably well informed and reasonably observant and circumspect."[1]

The Directive further prohibits labelling that contains health claims relating to the prevention, treatment or cure of human disease. Labelling must be in a format that is easy for the consumer to understand and, to this effect, Member States, especially those that are bilingual, can impose language requirements. Member States are entitled under the Directive to prohibit sales of foods whose labels do not appear in a language that can be easily understood by their consumers.

In accordance with the principle of the free movement of goods, Member States are prohibited by the Directive from using national barriers to stop trade in foods within the EU that comply with the Labelling Directive. However, this provision is subject to a safeguard clause, which allows Member States to derogate from the Directive on grounds of public health, prevention of fraud and protection of industrial and commercial

---

[1] See Case C-465/98 *Verein gegen Unwesen Handel und Gewerbe Koln eV v Adolf Darbo*; and also Case C-51/94 *Commission v Germany*.

property rights. In so doing, the Member State is required to notify the Commission and other Member States of the protection measures envisaged and give reasons justifying them. The Commission or any other Member State may ask for the Standing Committee on Foodstuffs to deliver opinion on the derogation. The Member State is only allowed to take such a measure 3 months after the date of notification provided that the Commission's opinion is not negative[2].

Article 3 of the Directive lists the information that must be displayed on the labelling of foodstuffs. Each requirement will be considered in turn.

7.2.1   The name under which the product is sold[3]

The general rule is that the name under which a foodstuff is sold should be the same as the name that is used for the particular foodstuff in Community legislation that applies to it. In the absence of any such Community legislation, the name used should be as provided for by the laws of the importing Member State. Failing national regulation, the name used should be the "name customary in the Member State in which it is sold to the final consumer or to mass caterers, or a description of the foodstuff, and if necessary of its use, which is clear enough to let the purchaser know its true nature and distinguish it from other products with which it might be confused."

Additionally, the use in the Member State in which the foodstuff is sold of the sales name under which the product is legally manufactured and marketed in the Member State of production is permissible. However, if the use of the sales name in the Member State of production could lead to confusion as to its identity in the eyes of the consumer in the Member State in which it is sold, the sales name should be accompanied by other descriptive information. Exceptionally, the same selling name shall not be used in cases where the risk of misleading the consumer as to the

---

[2] Such safeguard clauses are commonly found in Directives whose two-fold aim is to assure consumer protection whilst preserving the free movement of goods in the internal market.
[3] See Article 5

composition or manufacture of the product concerned is too great – for example where identical selling names in two Member States connote substantially different products.

No trade mark, brand name or fancy name may be substituted for the name under which the product is sold. The name under which the product is sold shall include particulars as to the physical condition of the foodstuff or the physical treatment that it has undergone (e.g. freeze-dried, deep-frozen, concentrated, smoked) in all cases where omission of such information could create confusion in the eyes of the purchaser. And, finally, any treatment of a foodstuff with ionising radiation must be indicated.

7.2.2   The list of ingredients

Ingredients shall be listed as required by Article 6 and Annexes I, II and III of the Directive.

Ingredient is defined in Article 6(4) as "any substance, including additives, used in the manufacture or preparation of a foodstuff and still present in the finished product, even if in altered form." Importantly, Article 6 further clarifies that, where an ingredient of the foodstuff is itself the product of several ingredients (i.e. a "compound ingredient"), it is the component ingredients that are to be regarded as the ingredients of the foodstuff in question. But, where the compound ingredient constitutes less than 25% of the finished product, it is not required by the Directive to be listed on the list of ingredients[4].   *Products within Products*

The following are not regarded as ingredients for the purposes of the Directive: the constituents of an ingredient that have been temporarily separated during manufacture and later reintroduced in similar proportions; additives whose presence in a foodstuff is solely due to the fact that they were contained in one or more of its ingredients and which do not serve a technological function in the finished product; additives that are used as processing aids; and substances used in the quantities strictly necessary as

---

[4] The 25% threshold is destined to be removed by the Commission's draft proposal to amend the Labelling Directive. See further at para 7.3 of this chapter.

solvents or media for additives or flavouring. Ingredients should appear on the label in descending order of weight, as recorded at the time of their use in the manufacture of the foodstuff.

Article 6(2) lists those ingredients that need not appear on foodstuff labelling. These include fresh fruit and vegetables that have not been peeled or treated; cheese, butter, fermented milk and cream to which no other (save for a few exceptions – e.g. lactic products) ingredient has been added; and products where the trade name is identical with the ingredient name or enables the ingredient to be clearly identified.

Annex I specifies categories of ingredients that may be designated by the name of the category rather than the specific ingredient name. The list includes: refined oils other than olive oil; refined fats; mixtures of flour obtained from two or more cereal species; starches; all species of fish where the fish constitutes an ingredient of another foodstuff; all types of cheese where the cheese or mixture of cheeses constitutes an ingredient of another foodstuff; sucrose; cocoa butter; wine; and mixtures of vegetables not exceeding 10% of the weight of the foodstuff. Annex II lists categories of ingredients that must be designated by their category followed by their specific name or EC number. These include: colour; preservative; thickener; gelling agent; sweetener and raising agent. Annex III concerns the designation of flavourings, which must be designated by the word "flavouring", or by a more specific description.

7.2.3   The quantity of ingredients[5]

It is compulsory for the quantity of an ingredient or category of ingredient to be stated on foodstuff labelling if the foodstuff meets one of the four following criteria:

i)   Where the ingredient or category of ingredient concerned appears in the name under which the foodstuff is sold (e.g. "mushroom pizza" or

---

[5] See Article 7 and, for further guidance, the "General Guidelines for implementing the principle of Quantitative Ingredients Declaration (QUID)", published by the Commission on 21 December 1998 and accessible from the D.G. Sanco Web site.

"fish fingers") or is usually associated with that name by the consumer (e.g. "chilli con carne", in which case the quantity of minced beef would have to be given, or "cassoulet" in which case the quantity of meat would have to be given).

ii)   Where the ingredient or category of ingredient is emphasised on the labelling in words, pictures or graphics. This provision will apply to products that state "with chicken", for example, or those that use a picture of a cow to emphasise dairy ingredients.

iii) Where the ingredient or category of ingredients concerned is essential to characterise a foodstuff and to distinguish it from products with which it might be confused because of its name or appearance. The range of foods likely to be affected is very narrow, as the provision is intended to cover products whose composition can differ markedly from one Member State to another. As at 1998, the only two foods that fell within this category were mayonnaise and marzipan.

iv)   In any case decided by the Standing Committee on Foodstuffs.

The quantity should appear either in or immediately next to the name under which the foodstuff is sold or in the list of ingredients.

The exceptions to the above requirements are listed at Article 7(3) and include the following: where the quantities are already required to be listed by other Community legislation; ingredients used in small amounts for flavouring (e.g. garlic, herbs and spices); and where the quantity of an ingredient mentioned in the name of a food does not affect the consumer's purchasing decision. With reference to the last exception, the Commission and the Member States have agreed a non-exhaustive list of products including malt whisky/whisky, liqueurs, fruit-based spirits and rye bread prepared exclusively with rye flour.

7.2.4 The net quantity of pre-packaged foodstuffs[6]

Subject to permissible derogations under other Community or national provisions, the Directive requires the net quantity of pre-packaged foodstuffs to be expressed for liquids in units of volume and for all other products in units of mass. The prescribed units of measurement are the litre, centilitre, millilitre, kilogram or gram as appropriate. In the case of foodstuffs that are sold by number, however, Member States are not required to indicate the net quantity provided that the number if items can clearly be seen and counted from the outside.

Where a solid foodstuff is presented in a liquid medium, the drained net weight of the foodstuff should also be indicated on the labelling. For these purposes, "liquid medium" means water, aqueous solutions of salts, brine, aqueous solutions of food acids, vinegar, aqueous solutions of sugars, aqueous solutions of other sweetening substances, and fruit or vegetable juices in the case of fruit and vegetables, provided that the liquid is merely an adjunct to the essential elements of the preparation and is thus not a decisive factor for the purchase.

Article 8(5) concerns the net quantity of foodstuffs that are either subject to considerable losses in their volume or mass and which are sold by number or weighed in the presence of the purchaser, or the net quantity of which is less than 5 g or 5 ml. In such circumstances, it is not compulsory for producers to indicate the net quantity. This exemption does not apply to herbs and spices.

Finally, in relation to pre-packaged foodstuffs, the Directive provides[7] that the list of particulars required by Article 3 should be conspicuously, clearly and indelibly indicated either on the pre-packaging or on a label attached to it. However, as an exception to this, where the prepackaged foodstuffs are marketed at a stage prior to sale to the ultimate consumer and where sale to a mass caterer is not involved at that stage, or are supplied to mass caterers for preparation and processing, the list of particulars, with the

---

[6] See Article 8
[7] See Article 13

94

exception of the product name, the date of minimum durability and the business name and address of the manufacturer/packager/seller, need only appear on the commercial documents accompanying the foodstuff.

7.2.5 The date of minimum durability/use-by date and storage conditions[8]

The date of minimum durability is defined as the date "until which the foodstuff retains its specific properties when properly stored." If need be, the date may be accompanied by a description of the storage conditions that must be observed if the product is to keep for the specified period. The date should be preceded by "best before" if it includes the day and "best before end" if it includes the month and/or year. In the case of foodstuffs that will not keep for more than 3 months, an indication of the day and the month will suffice. In the case of foodstuffs that will keep for between 3 and 18 months, an indication of the month and year will suffice. In the case of foodstuffs that will keep for over 18 months, an indication of the year will suffice. "Best before" dates are not required for untreated fresh fruit and vegetables, wines, beverages containing 10% or more by volume of alcohol, soft drinks, fruit juices, fruit nectars and alcoholic beverages in individual containers of more than 5 litres, intended for supply to mass caterers, pastries that, given their content, are normally eaten within 24 hours of their manufacture, vinegar, cooking salt, solid sugar, confectionery products consisting almost solely of flavoured and/or coloured sugars, chewing gums and individual portions of ice cream.

Perishable foodstuffs that are likely to present a danger to health if not consumed within a short period must have a "use by" date indicated on their labelling. This should also be accompanied by a description of the storage conditions that should be observed. Furthermore, the instructions for storage and use of a foodstuff should be clearly indicated so as not to confuse or mislead the consumer.

---

[8] See Articles 9, 10 and 11

7.2.6   Business names and addresses

The label should present the name or business name and address of the manufacturer/packager/seller established within the Community; particulars of the place of origin where its omission might lead consumers to a material degree as to the true origin of the foodstuff.

7.2.7   Alcoholic strength of beverages

In the case of beverages containing more than 1.2% by volume of alcohol, the actual alcoholic strength by volume should be stated[9].

7.3   Commission Proposal (06.09.2001 COM (2001) 433 Final) to Amend the Labelling Directive

In the White Paper on Food Safety, the Commission announced its intention to amend the Labelling Directive 2000/13/EC by making it compulsory to label the ingredients of all compound ingredients. At present, only the ingredients of compound ingredients that constitute over 25% of the finished product have to be listed. The Explanatory Memorandum to the proposal explains the reason for the amendment as being that, (as food production has become more complex and people eat much more processed foods, so consumers need to be better informed about the foodstuffs they purchase, even if full ingredients labelling will inevitably make ingredient lists longer.)The Commission also cites the recent food scares as further justification for better information for consumers.

The Proposal also addresses the issue of food allergens. Based principally on the findings of the Scientific Committee for Food, which concluded that the incidence of food allergy is such as to seriously affect the lives of many people in the EU, the Commission considers that consumers with allergies should be better protected by more comprehensive information about the composition of foodstuffs they eat. The Proposal seeks

---

[9] The labelling of ingredients on alcoholic beverages (i.e. with more than 1.2% by volume of alcohol) is not as yet regulated at EU level. Commission proposal (Com 97(20)) requires ingredients labelling for such alcoholic beverages and is currently being considered by the European Parliament and the Council.

therefore to amend the Labelling Directive by ensuring that all known allergens are specifically declared by their name on labels of foodstuffs and alcoholic drinks, thereby not allowing any possibility for their presence to be obscured by using the name of the category to which they belong, or, in the case of additives, any exemption from inclusion in the list of ingredients. The list of allergens covers: cereals containing gluten and their products; crustaceans and their products; eggs and their products; fish and their products; peanuts and their products; soya beans and their products; milk and dairy products (including lactose); nuts and nut products; sesame seeds and their products; and sulfate at concentrations of at least 10 mg/kg.

7.4   The Nutrition Labelling Directive (90/496/EEC)

The twin objective of this Directive is to promote free movement of goods in the internal market by laying down common rules on nutrition labelling and, of equal importance, to improve nutrition education for the public. The recitals to the Directive acknowledge that "there is growing public interest in the relationship between diet and health and in the choice of an appropriate diet to suit individual needs...[and that] knowledge of the basic principles of nutrition and appropriate nutrition labelling of foodstuffs would contribute significantly towards enabling the consumer to make this choice."

The Directive concerns nutrition labelling of foodstuffs intended for the individual consumer and restaurants, hospitals, canteens or other similar mass caterers. It does not apply to natural mineral waters or other waters intended for human consumption, which are the subject of a separate Directive; nor does it apply to diet integrators or food supplements that are regulated by other Directives[10].

Nutrition labelling is defined as "any information appearing on labelling and relating to: (i) energy value; and (ii) the following nutrients: protein, carbohydrate, fat, fibre, sodium, vitamins and minerals (as listed in the Annex to the Directive with their recommended daily allowances)".

---

[10] See Chapter 10

Nutrition labelling is not compulsory unless a nutrition claim is made on the product itself or in advertising material; in other words, a producer is not automatically required by this Directive to list nutritional content. A nutrition claim is defined as: any representation and any advertising message that states, suggests or implies that a foodstuff has particular nutrition properties due to the energy (calorific value) it

- provides,
- provides at a reduced or increased rate, or
- does not provide,

and/or due to the nutrients it

- contains,
- contains in reduced or increased proportions, or
- does not contain.

The scope for making nutrition claims on labels under EU legislation is at present very restrictive. The only nutrition claims that are permitted by this Directive are those relating to energy value and to the nutrients listed above. But where nutrition labelling is provided, the information to be given shall consist of the amount of protein, carbohydrate, sugars, fat, saturates, fibre or sodium. Nutrition labelling can also include the amounts of starch, polyols, mono-unsaturates, polyunsaturates, cholesterol and any of the vitamins and mineral listed in the Annex and present in significant amounts. The declared energy value and amount of nutrients shall be given in figures using specific units of measurement expressed per 100 g or 100 ml per package.

All of the above information should be grouped together in a clearly visible place on the product and should be written legibly and indelibly in a language that can be easily understood by the purchaser. Member States are not permitted to introduce nutrition labelling specifications that are more detailed than those contained in this Directive.

7.5   Nutritional and Functional Claims

In the White Paper[11], the Commission states that it will consider whether specific provisions should be introduced in EU law to govern "functional claims" (claims related to the beneficial effects of a nutrient on certain normal bodily functions) and "nutritional claims". To this end the Commission has published a Discussion Paper[12], which solicited responses from interested parties by 20 July 2001. Developing a coherent policy on the nutritional value of food is one of the Commission's primary objectives.

The Discussion Paper notes in its introduction that consumers have become increasingly interested in their diet, its relationship to their health, and, more generally, the composition of foods they are eating. It also notes that the food industry has responded to this increased interest by providing nutritional labelling on many foods. Because of the proliferation of the number and type of claims appearing on the labels of foodstuffs that are imported into the EU, some Member States have adopted legislation to regulate their use, with the result that many discrepancies exist within the Community. The Commission is therefore of the view that rules regarding such claims should be harmonised in order to "reach the twin objective of achieving both the free movement of foodstuffs between Member States and a high level of consumer protection". It does not, however, advocate that claims relating to the prevention, treatment or cure of human disease, currently prohibited under the Labelling Directive, should be permitted if substantiated. The Discussion Paper invites particular comments on the question of definitions, conditions under which claims may be made and the type of evaluation systems for claims.

Based on the comments received, the Commission services will prepare a proposal for Community legislation on this subject. This is an area in which further legislation can be expected shortly.

---

[11] Para 101
[12] SANCO/1341/2001 - the Discussion Paper and responses are available from the D.G. Sanco Web Site

7.6   Further Directives with Labelling Requirements

There are further Directives incorporating labelling requirements, which will be considered in later chapters. Two Directives, however, merit mention here.

Council Directive 89/108/EEC on the approximation of laws of the Member States relating to quick-frozen foodstuffs for human consumption requires the labelling of quick-frozen foods to include the sales name, the indication "quick-frozen", and the batch identification. Furthermore, if the product is intended for ultimate consumers, restaurants, hospitals and canteens, the date of minimum durability must be displayed, as must the period during which the product may be stored.

Regulation 1760/2000/EC of the Parliament and Council, establishing a system for the identification and registration of bovine animals, reinforces from 1 January 2002 onwards the compulsory beef labelling system that was introduced after the BSE crisis by Council Regulation 820/97/EC, as amended. Operations and organisations marketing beef in the Community have to indicate on the labelling the following information:

i)   a reference number or reference code ensuring the link between the meat and the animal or animals;

ii)   the approval number of the slaughterhouse at which the animal or group of animals were slaughtered and the Member State or third country in which the slaughterhouse is established; and

iii)   the approval number of the cutting hall that performed the cutting operation on the carcass and the Member State in which the hall is established.

In addition, they should also indicate on the label information concerning origin, in particular where the animals were born, fattened and slaughtered. For operators in third countries importing beef into the EU, each operator should obtain the approval of the competent authority in the country of export, such approval being subject to further approval by the Commission before beef can be imported to the Community. Finally, labelling on minced beef must contain a traceability code, Member State of slaughter, Member State of preparation, and Member State of origin.

7.7   Conclusion

Food labelling regulation in the EU has long served twin objectives: that of assuring the smooth running of the internal market; and that of the protection of consumer health. To this end, the current Labelling Directive goes a long way in consolidating and clarifying the law of food labelling in one "Framework" Directive. Once amended, it will cover all ingredients and known allergens. But, of the twin objectives served, it has become clear over recent years, and particularly since the series of food crises starting with BSE, that consumer health is now by far the most prominent. Consumers now want to know far more about the contents of the food they are eating and its relationship with their health. This will put an increasing strain on food producers to squeeze more and more information onto labels, to the extent that they may become too complex to read easily, thereby defeating the ultimate purpose of the label. The Commission is aware of this impending problem - a growing tension between the desire of the consumer to be better informed and the finite amount of space available on food labels - but has not yet decided how to respond. It is noteworthy that, in the tenth recital to its proposal to amend the Labelling Directive, the Commission states:

"In order to avoid the risk that labelling may become too complex and difficult to read, procedures are needed which make it possible to avoid excessively long lists of ingredients, but without impairing the attainment of the above-mentioned objectives. In order to take account of the technical constraints involved in the manufacture of foodstuffs, it is also necessary to authorise greater flexibility with regard to the listing of ingredients used in very small quantities".

Commissioner Byrne took up this theme in some of his speeches last year in Brussels. He has commented with approval on the fact that many food producers already make available through their Web sites and other means significant amounts of consumer information. He has publicly asked whether the Commission should be encouraging more enterprises to "go down this road to satisfy consumer demand?"[13] The Commission is currently consulting on this topic, which will have to be resolved if consumer demand for more detailed information is to be met.

---

[13] Round Table on Food and Agriculture, Brussels 26 July 2001

8. COMPOSITIONAL REQUIREMENTS

8.1 Introduction

There are a number of Directives, mostly adopted in the 1970s, whose purpose was to facilitate the free movement of certain foodstuffs by harmonising national provisions relating to their composition and manufacturing specifications. Each will be of particular relevance to those manufacturers or retailers producing and marketing the products that that particular Directive regulates. It is not, however, within the scope of this work to set out the detailed requirements of each Directive; instead, this chapter will review the contents of those Directives that are likely to be of the greatest relevance to users of this book, and then will list further product-specific Directives relating to compositional requirements[1].

8.2 Cocoa and Chocolate

8.2.1 Directive 73/241/EEC on cocoa and chocolate products intended for human consumption, as amended

The preamble to this Directive specifies that it is necessary to lay down definitions and common rules in respect of the composition, manufacturing specifications, packaging and labelling of cocoa and chocolate products in order to ensure their free movement. It recognises that the use of vegetable fats other than cocoa butter in chocolate products is permitted in certain Member States but not in others; but it does not adopt any Community-wide specifications on the use of vegetable fats owing to "an absence of sufficient economic and technical data". The preamble further suggests that the situation should be re-examined in the light of future developments. But it was not until 2000, 27 years later, that Directive 2000/36/EC laid down, after much dispute, maximum quantities applicable in all Member States for the use of vegetable fats in the manufacture of cocoa and chocolate.

---

[1] All of which can be easily accessed from "Eur-Lex" on the EU Web site www.europa.eu.int/eur-lex

The first Directive defines cocoa and chocolate products as being limited to the products listed in Annex I to the Directive. For each product listed in the Annex, there is a definition recorded underneath. The products listed in the Annex are: cocoa beans, cocoa nib, cocoa dust and fines, cocoa mass, cocoa press cake, fat-reduced cocoa press cake, cocoa powder, fat-reduced cocoa powder, sweetened cocoa, sweetened cocoa powder, drinking chocolate, sweetened fat-reduced cocoa and cocoa powder, fat-reduced drinking chocolate, cocoa butter, cocoa fat, chocolate, plain chocolate, Vermicelli chocolate, chocolate flakes, Gianduja nut chocolate, couverture chocolate, milk chocolate, milk chocolate with high milk content, milk chocolate Vermicelli, milk chocolate flakes, couverture milk chocolate, white chocolate, and filled chocolate.

Article 10 prohibits Member States from impeding trade in these products by the application of national non-harmonised provisions, except in cases of protection of public health, repression of fraud and protection of industrial and commercial property, indications of source, applications of origin and repression of unfair competition (i.e. when the safeguard clause is invoked).

The Directive stipulates that cocoa beans that are not sound, wholesome and in good market condition, shells, germs or any other residual products from the solvent-extraction of cocoa butter may not be used in the manufacture of any of the products defined in Annex I. It further specifies that chocolate that is manufactured in the form of bars should be marketed in the following individual weights: 85 g, 100 g, 125 g, 150 g, 200 g, 250 g, 300 g, 400 g and 500 g.

The following labelling information should appear on the packaging of all the products listed in Annex I:

i) the names listed in Annex I(1) should be used only for the products defined in that paragraph and must be used in trade to designate them; certain derogations apply to the names "pralina" and "cioccolatino" in Italy, "a chocolate" in Ireland and England, "milk chocolate" in Ireland and England, and "filled chocolate" in Ireland and England;

ii)   for certain cocoa products, an indication of the total dry cocoa content by the declaration "cocoa solids...% minimum";

iii) for filled chocolates obtained from chocolate products other than chocolate and couverture chocolate, an additional indication of the types of chocolate used;

iv)   the net weight, unless the products weigh less than 50 g;

v)   the name or trade name and the address or registered office of the manufacturer and packer, or of a seller established within the Community;

vi)   for products in packages and containers holding a net weight of not less than 10 kg which are not retailed, the labelling information listed above may appear in the accompanying documents.

vii) the name "chocolate" and "milk chocolate" may be supplemented by declarations or adjectives relating to quality only if:

–   the chocolate has a total dry cocoa solids content of at least 43%, including at least 26% cocoa butter;

–   the milk chocolate contains not more than 50% sucrose and at least 30% total dry cocoa solids, and 18% milk solids obtained by evaporation, including at least 4.5% butterfat.

8.2.2   Directive 2000/36/EC on cocoa and chocolate products intended for human consumption

This Directive repeals and simplifies Directive 73/24/EEC taking account of only the essential requirements to be met by cocoa and chocolate products in order that they may move freely within the internal market[2]. Provisions concerning permissible quantities of vegetable fat other than cocoa butter in chocolate products proved to be divisive, and agreement was reached only after much delay. The Directive will not come into force before 3 August 2003.

---

[2] In accordance with the conclusions of the European Council held in Edinburgh in December 1992

The second Directive applies to the cocoa and chocolate products listed in Annex 1 to the Directive. The definitions in this Annex amend those of the 1973 Directive by taking account of technological progress and changes in consumer taste. Sales names and definitions are provided for cocoa butter, cocoa powder and cocoa, chocolate, milk chocolate, family milk chocolate, white chocolate, filled chocolate, chocolate a la taza, chocolate familiar a la taza, and a chocolate or a praline. The Annex further lists optional authorised ingredients, prescribes the manner of calculating percentages and defines "sugars" as referred to in the Directive.

Vegetable fats other than cocoa butter are defined in Annex II and are described as cocoa butter equivalents. Article 2 of the Directive specifies that vegetable fats that meet the criteria laid down in Annex II may be used in chocolate, milk chocolate, family milk chocolate, white chocolate, chocolate a la taza and chocolate familiar a la taza. The quantity of vegetable fat must not exceed 5% of the finished product. Such products may then be marketed in all of the Member States, provided that their labelling is supplemented by the following conspicuous and clearly legible statement: "contains vegetable fats in addition to cocoa butter".

The Labelling Directive 2000/13/EC now applies to the products listed in Annex I, subject to the further requirements of the 1973 Directive (set out above and repeated in this Directive) and the following further requirements:

i) Where products are sold in assortments, the sales names may be replaced by "assorted chocolates" or "assorted filled chocolates" or similar names. In such cases there may be a single list of ingredients for all the products in the assortment.

ii) The sales names "chocolate", "milk chocolate" and "couverture chocolate" specified in Annex I may be supplemented by information or descriptions relating to quality criteria, provided that the products contain:

- in the case of chocolate, not less than 43% total dry cocoa solids, including not less than 26% cocoa butter;
- in the case of milk chocolate, not less than 30% total dry cocoa solids and not less than 18% dry milk solids obtained by partly or wholly dehydrating whole milk, semi- or full-skimmed milk, cream, or from partly or wholly dehydrated cream, butter or milk fat, including not less than 4.5% milk fat;
- in the case of couverture chocolate, not less than 16% of dry, non-fat cocoa solids.

The marketing of products that were labelled before 3 August 2003 (when the new chocolate Directive comes into force) and which comply with the requirements of the 1973 Directive will be permitted after 3 August 2003 until stocks are exhausted.

Member States are required to transpose this Directive into their national legal systems before 3 August 2003. Subject to the derogation for labelling of old stocks (above), Member States will be required from that date onwards to allow trade in cocoa and chocolate products that conform with the provisions of this Directive and prohibit trade in those products that do not.

8.3   Sugars Intended for Human Consumption

8.3.1   *Directive 73/437/EEC on certain sugars intended for human onsumption*

The purpose of this Directive was to ensure the smooth running of the common organisation of the market in sugar (sucrose) by regulating various quality and compositional requirements for this type of product and prescribing labelling and packaging rules.

Article 1 of the Directive lists the specific compositional and quality requirements for the following products: semi-white sugar, sugar or white sugar, extra white sugar, sugar solution, invert sugar solution, invert sugar syrup, glucose syrup, dried glucose syrup, dextrose monohydrate, dextrose anhydrous. The Directive does not apply to impalpable sugars, candy sugars, and sugars in loaf form. An example of the requirements listed would be, in the case of semi-white sugar:

> "means purified and crystallised sucrose, of sound and fair marketable quality with the following characteristics:
>
> (a) polarisation: not less than 99.5%
>
> (b) invert sugar content: not more than 0.10% by weight
>
> (c) loss in drying: not more than 0.10% by weight
>
> (d) residual sulphur   not more than 15 mg/kg
>   dioxide content"[3]

Member States are required to ensure that the products listed in Article 1 are offered for sale only if they comply with the definitions and criteria laid down in that Article and not to prohibit their sale if they do.

The names listed in Article 1 shall be applied only to the products meeting the relevant definition and must be used in trade to designate them. The description "white" is reserved:

(a) for sugar solution where the colour in the solution does not exceed 25 ICUMSA[4] units, determined in accordance with the Annex to the Directive

(b) for invert sugar solution and for invert sugar syrup, of which:

– the ash content does not exceed 0.1%

– the colour in solution does not exceed 25 ICUMSA units determined in accordance with the Annex to the Directive.

---

[3] See Article 1(1)

[4] As calculated by the method of the International Commission for Uniform Methods of Sugar Analysis (ICUMSA).

The Directive imposes selling weights for semi-white sugar, sugar or white sugar and extra white sugar. Such products should only be offered for sale at the following individual net weights: 125 g, 250 g, 500 g, 750 g, 1 kg, 1.5 kg, 2 kg, 2.5 kg, 3 kg, 4 kg and 5 kg.

The following labelling requirements are imposed by the Directive:

i)   the qualifying expression "includes colouring agents" is obligatory in the description of products containing colouring agents, and the term "white" will therefore not apply;

ii) the net weight unless the products weigh less than 50 g;

iii) the name and trade name and the address or registered office of the manufacturer or packer, or of a seller established within the Community;

iv) an indication of the true content of dry matter and invert sugar in the case of sugar solution, and invert sugar syrup;

v)   the qualifying term "crystallised" for invert sugar syrup incorporating crystals in the solution;

The above specifications should be conspicuous, clearly legible and indelible. A derogation to some of the above requirements is made for packages of products exceeding 10 kg in weight not being offered for retail sale.

8.4   Honey

8.4.1   Directive 74/409/EEC relating to honey

The purpose of this Directive was to define the term honey, to make provision for the different varieties that may be marketed, to fix the general specific criteria for its composition, and to lay down the main information that is to appear on labels.

Under the terms of this Directive, honey means "the foodstuff which is produced by the honey-bee from the nectar of blossoms or secretions of or on living parts of plants, and which the bees collect, transform, combine with specific substances of their own and leave to mature in honey combs. This foodstuff may be fluid, viscous or crystallised."[5] Member States are required only to permit the sale of honey if it complies with the provisions of this Directive.

Article 1 of the Directive lists the main types of honey as being: (according to origin) blossom honey, honeydew honey; (according to mode of presentation) comb honey, chunk honey, drained honey, extracted honey and pressed honey. Each of those names is accompanied by a definition.

When honey is sold, it has to comply with the compositional criteria that are listed in the Annex to the Directive (exceptions are made for heather honey and bakers' honey). In addition, honey should be free from organic and inorganic matters that are foreign to its composition (e.g. mould and insect débris). Nor should it have any foreign tastes or odours, have begun to ferment or effervesce, have been heated to such an extent that its natural enzymes are destroyed or made inactive, or have an artificially changed acidity. The Directive further stipulates that no product other than honey can be added to honey offered for sale as such.

There are labelling requirements to use, *inter alia*, the trade names given in Article 1, to express the weight in grams or kilograms, and to include the name and address of the producer, packer or seller. Exception to the above is made for "honeydew" honey and for packages of over 10 kg, in which case the information can appear on the accompanying documentation.

8.5   Dehydrated Preserved Milk

8.5.1   *Directive 76/118/EEC relating to partly or wholly dehydrated preserved milk for human consumption*

The Directive applies to partly or wholly dehydrated preserved milk as defined in the Annex. "Partly dehydrated milk" is defined as the liquid product obtained directly by the partial removal of water from milk, from

---

[5] See Article 1

wholly or partly skimmed milk, or from a mixture of these products. "Wholly dehydrated milk" means the solid product, whose moisture content is not more than 5% by weight of the finished product obtained directly by the removal of water from milk, wholly or partly skimmed milk, cream or from a mixture of these products. The Directive does not apply to dietetic products or products specifically prepared for babies and young children[6].

The Annex lists designations and definitions for the following partly dehydrated milks: unsweetened condensed milk, unsweetened condensed skimmed milk, unsweetened condensed partly skimmed milk, unsweetened condensed high-fat milk, sweetened condensed milk, sweetened condensed skimmed milk and unsweetened condensed partly skimmed milk. It also lists designations and definitions for the following wholly dehydrated milks: dried whole milk or whole milk powder, dried skimmed milk or skimmed milk powder, dried partly skimmed milk or partly skimmed milk powder and dried high-fat milk or high-fat milk powder. The preservation of these products is achieved by sterilisation, by the addition of sucrose or by dehydration, depending on the product.

Article 5 lists in detail the ingredients that are permitted in the manufacture of the products listed in the Annex.

The general labelling Directive (2000/13/EC) applies to the sale of the products listed in the Annex to the ultimate consumer. The following information should also appear on the label or packaging:

i)   the percentage of milk fat, expressed by weight in relation to the finished product, except in the case of unsweetened condensed skimmed milk, sweetened condensed skimmed milk and dried skimmed milk or skimmed milk powder, and the percentage of fat-free dried milk extract in the case of the products falling under the definition of "partly dehydrated milk";

---

[6] These are considered in Chapter 10

ii) for products falling under the definition of "partly dehydrated milk", the recommendations on the method of dilution or reconstitution; these particulars may be replaced by relevant information on the use of the products when the latter are intended for use in the unaltered state;

iii) in the case of products falling under the definition of "wholly dehydrated milk", the recommendations on the method of dilution or reconstitution, including details of the fat content of the product thus diluted or reconstituted, except for dried skimmed milk or skimmed milk powder;

iv) the expression "UHT" or "ultra heat treated" for unsweetened condensed milk, unsweetened condensed skimmed milk, unsweetened condensed partly skimmed milk, and unsweetened condensed high-fat milk.

All the products referred to in Article 1 and destined for retail sale must be packaged in sealed containers.

In the case of labelling on products that are not intended for the ultimate consumer, the Directive imposes the following mandatory requirements, which should be visibly labelled:

i) the name reserved for these products;

ii) the net quantity expressed in kilograms or grams;

iii) the name and business address of the manufacturer, packer or seller established within the Community;

iv) the name of the country of origin if imported into the Community from a third country;

v) the date of manufacture or some marking by which the batch can be identified.

Finally, Member States are obliged to permit trade in these products if they comply with the terms of this Directive.

8.6   Fruit Jams, Jellies, Marmalades and Sweetened Chestnut Purée

8.6.1   Directive 79/693/EEC relating to fruit jams, jellies, marmalades and sweetened chestnut purée

This Directive, as with the other Directives listed above, was intended to establish common rules for these products in order to facilitate their free movement within the Community. Member States are therefore required not to prohibit trade in these products that complies with the terms of this Directive.

The Directive applies to "extra jam, jam, extra jelly, jelly, marmalade and sweetened chestnut purée". Annex 1 to the Directive provides a definition for each of these products. Article 3 states that the names listed in Annex 1 should be used exclusively to denote the products defined therein; accordingly, they should be sold under that name. In Annex II are listed the raw materials that are permitted to be used in the manufacture of the products defined in Annex I, and in Annex III are listed the substances (edible ingredients, aromatics, and additives) that are permitted to be added to the products defined in Annex I. However, Article 15 contains a list of substances that may be added to these products under national provisions as an exception to the requirements of Annex III. The maximum sulfur dioxide content for the products regulated by this Directive are contained in the final Annex, Annex IV. Finally, the Directive does not apply to dietetic products, or to products intended for the manufacture of fine bakers' wares, pastries and biscuits.

The labelling requirements are governed by the current Labelling Directive, subject to the following further requirements.

The name under which these products is sold should be supplemented by:

−   an indication of the type or types of fruit used in descending order by weight of the raw materials used; however, for products made from three or more types of fruit, the indication of the types of fruit may be replaced by the words "mixed fruit" or by an indication of the number of types of fruit used;

- an indication of the ingredients listed in Annex III(A)(2) (substances that may be added);
- where apricots dried in a process other than freeze drying are used in jam, the words "dried apricots" shall appear in the list of ingredients;
- where red beetroot juice has been added to jam and jelly made from strawberries, raspberries, gooseberries, redcurrants or plums, the words "red beetroot juice to reinforce the colour" shall appear in the list of ingredients;
- in the case of products made from three or more types of fruit, Member States may allow the naming in the list of ingredients of the types of fruit used by the single word "fruit";
- where the residual sulfur dioxide content is more than 30 mg/kg, the words "sulfur dioxide" shall appear in the list of ingredients according to the percentage by weight of the residue in the finished product.

The labelling of the products defined in Annex 1 should also bear the following obligatory information:

- the words "prepared with....g of fruit per 100 g",
- the words "total sugar content....g per 100 g"
- for products having a soluble dry matter content of less than 63% the words "keep in a cool place once opened"
- for marmalade:
  - containing peel, an indication of the style of cut of that peel;
  - not containing peel, an indication of the absence of peel.

In relation to products that are not destined for the final consumer, the Directive leaves regulation of such products to the Member States.

8.7   Further Directives

The following Regulations and Directives may be of relevance to food and drink operators:

Regulation 1601/91/EEC laying down general rules on the definition, description and presentation of aromatized wines, aromatised wine-based drinks and aromatised wine-product cocktails, as amended by Regulation 3279/92/EEC, Regulation 122/94/EC, Regulation 3378/94/EC and Regulation 2061/96/EC.

Regulation 1576/89/EEC laying down general rules on the definition, description and presentation of spirit drinks, as amended by Regulation 3378/94/EC.

Directive 80/777/EEC relating to the exploitation and marketing of natural mineral waters, as amended by Directive 80/1276/EEC, Directive 85/7/EEC and Directive 96/70/EC.

Directive 1999/4/EC relating to coffee extracts and chicory extracts

Directive 1993/77/EEC relating to fruit juices and similar products

Directive 93/45/EEC concerning the manufacture of nectars without the addition of sugars and honey

Directive 78/142/EEC relating to materials and articles which contain vinyl chloride monomer and are intended to come into contact with foodstuffs

Directive 88/344/EEC on extraction solvents used in the production of foodstuffs and food ingredients

Directive 89/109/EEC relating to materials and articles intended to come into contact with foodstuffs.

9. FOOD ADDITIVES AND FLAVOURING

9.1 Food Additives

A food additive is defined as "any substance not normally consumed as a food in itself and not normally used as a characteristic ingredient of food whether or not it has nutritive value, the intentional addition of which to foods for a technological purpose in the manufacture, processing, preparation, treatment, packaging, transport or storage of such foods results, or may be reasonably expected to result, in it or its by-products becoming directly or indirectly a component of such foods."[1] Typical examples of additives are preservatives, colourings and sweeteners.

Under the EU's programme of harmonisation of national legislation, only additives that have been evaluated by the Scientific Committee for Food and authorised by the Commission in a regulatory Committee are permitted to be used within the EU. Those additives that are authorised for marketing and use appear in lists annexed to each of the relevant Directives (see below). If the additive is not listed, it is not authorised within the Community. Food additives will be authorised only if there is a technological need for their use, they present no hazard to the health of the consumer, and they do not mislead the consumer. Additionally, the majority of additives may only be used in specified quantities.

EU legislation as it relates to food additives is contained in one framework Directive (Directive 89/107/EEC) either amended or supplemented by Directives 94/34/EC, 94/35/EC, 94/36/EC, 96/83/EC, 95/2/EC, 96/85/EC, 98/72/EC, and 2001/5/EC. The framework Directive and its three specific Directives, which together comprise the "comprehensive"[2] Directive on additives, will each be considered in turn.

---

[1] Article 1(2) of Directive 89/107/EEC
[2] See Article 3 of Directive 89/107/EEC

9.1.1 Directive 89/107/EEC on food additives authorised for use in foodstuffs intended for human consumption, as amended by Directive 94/34/EC

This framework Directive applies to the following categories of additives provided that they are used or intended to be used as ingredients during the manufacture or preparation of a foodstuff and are still present in the final product: colour, preservative, antioxidant, emulsifier, emulsifying salt, thickener, gelling agent, stabiliser (including foam stabiliser), flavour enhancer, acid, acidity regulator, anti-caking agent, modified starch, sweetener, raising agent, anti-foaming agent, glazing agent (including lubricants), flour treatment agent, firming agent, humectant, sequestrant, enzymes used as additives, bulking agent and propellant and packaging gas. Processing aids, substances used in the protection of plants, flavourings falling under Directive 88/388/EEC and substances added to foodstuffs as nutrients are not categories of additives under this Directive.

For each of the above categories, an exclusive list of approved additives is contained in the three specific Directives, which are considered below. Only those additives appearing on the relevant lists may be used in the manufacture or preparation of foodstuffs and only under the conditions specified therein.

Annex II sets out the general criteria for the approval of food additives and their inclusion in the relevant list for each category of additive. The Annex specifies that additives can be approved only where a reasonable technological need for their use can be demonstrated and where there is evidence that the proposed use of the additive would bring demonstrable benefits rather than risks to the consumer. In other words, for an additive to be authorised, it is necessary to establish the case for what is commonly referred to as "need". The annex lists four purposes, one or more of which must be served by food additives:

● to preserve the nutritional quality of the food: an intentional reduction in the nutritional quality of a food would be justified only where the food does not constitute a significant item in a normal diet or where the additive is necessary for the production of foods for groups of consumers having special dietary needs;

- to provide necessary ingredients or constituents for foods manufactured for groups of consumers having special dietary needs;

- to enhance the keeping quality or stability of a food or to improve its organoleptic properties, provided that this does not so change the nature, substance or quality of the food as to deceive the consumer;

- to provide aids in manufacture, processing, preparation, treatment, packing, transport or storage of food, provided that the additive is not used to disguise the effects of the use of faulty raw materials or of undesirable (including unhygienic) practices or techniques during the course of any of these activities.

Annex II further explains that approval for a food additive on the relevant list should specify the foodstuff to which the additive may be added and the conditions under which it may be added. Approval should also be limited to the lowest level of use necessary to achieve the desired effect. It is a further requirement that approval of an additive should take into account any acceptable intake threshold that has been established for the additive and the figure for the probable average daily intake of it from all sources. Where the food additive is to be used in foods eaten by special groups of consumers, additional account should be taken of the possible daily intake of the food additive by consumers in those groups. All additives must also comply with any criteria of purity that have been adopted by the Commission after consultation with the Standing Committee on foodstuffs[3].

A safeguard clause in the Directive allows a Member State temporarily to restrict the use of an EU-authorised food additive on the basis of new information or a reassessment of existing information concerning the risk to human health posed by the particular additive. For a unilateral suspension

---

[3] The detailed purity criteria for sweeteners are contained in Directive 95/31/EC, as amended by Directive 98/66/EC and 2000/51/EC; for colours are contained in Directive 95/45/EC, as amended by 99/75/EC; for additives other than colours and sweeteners are contained in Directive 96/86/EC and 2000/63/EC.

of the use of an additive to become permanent, the usual provisions requiring the approval of the measure by the Commission following consultation with the Scientific Committee on Foodstuffs apply.

Moreover, Member States are permitted by the Directive provisionally to authorise the use of an additive within their territory not appearing on a list if technical developments that have occurred since the adoption of the list recommend its authorisation. By such means, Member States are able to take advantage of scientific progress before the more time-consuming process of amending a list is completed. However, such authorisations are qualified by the following: they are limited to a maximum of 2 years; Member States are required officially to monitor all foodstuffs containing the additive; Member States may require that foodstuffs with the additive in question bear a special indication on the label; and such authorisations have to be communicated to the Commission and all other Member States. If the authorisation is not approved at Commission level within the 2-year period, or is not subsequently adopted by the Council of Ministers, the national authorisation will be cancelled.

The use of food additives – whether or not intended for sale to the ultimate consumer - must always be clearly labelled on the packaging of food products. The labelling requirements are set out in this Directive as supplemented by the Labelling Directive 2000/13/EC. They include the name under which the product is sold or E-number, the statement "for use/restricted use in food", if necessary directions and special conditions for use, a mark identifying the batch or lot, and the name and address of the manufacturer, packager or seller and the net quantity.

The framework Directive on food additives was amended by Directive 94/34/EC, which introduced limited derogation from the Community-wide requirement to allow the marketing and use of additives authorised at EU level in the case of certain specific foodstuffs considered by Member States to be "traditional". The amending Directive inserted Article 3a into the framework Directive, which allowed Member States to maintain the prohibition on the use of certain additives in the production of foodstuffs that they considered to be traditional provided that the prohibition existed on 1 January 1992, and provided that they authorised the production and sale of all other foodstuffs not considered as traditional. Member States were required to submit lists to the Commission of all traditional foodstuffs, with detailed reasons given in support of the prohibition, together with the relevant national legislative provisions. Among the list of derogations approved are *feta* cheese in Greece, traditional French bread, preserved truffles, preserved snails, and goose, duck and turkey confits in France.

The framework Directive on food additives has been supplemented by three specific Directives, which lay down further rules on the use of sweeteners, colouring and all other food additives. All four Directives constitute a "comprehensive" Directive on food additives within the meaning of Article 3 of the framework Directive.

9.1.2 Directive 94/35/EC on sweeteners for use in foodstuffs, as amended by Directive 96/83/EC

The Sweetener Directive recognises in its recitals that the use of sweeteners to replace sugar is justified:

- for the production of energy-reduced food, non-carcinogenic foodstuffs or food without added sugars,
- for the extension of shelf life through the replacement of sugar; and
- for the production of dietetic products.

But it is also concerned with the possible toxicological impact of sweeteners, and so its primary stated objective is "to protect and inform the consumer"[4], and this it achieves by prescribing which sweeteners are permitted for which foodstuffs and under which conditions.

The Directive applies to all sweeteners that are used to impart a sweet taste to foodstuffs or which are used as table-top sweeteners. It prohibits sweeteners from being used in food for infants and young children unless otherwise laid down by other Directives. It is therefore only the sweeteners

---

[4] See the eighth recital

listed in the Annex to the Directive that are allowed to be placed on the market within the Community either for sale to the ultimate consumer or for use in the manufacture of foodstuffs. Sweeteners that are intended for use in the manufacture of foodstuffs should additionally comply with the conditions for their use set out in the Annex.

The Annex comprises four columns headed, respectively, EC No./ Name/ Foodstuff/ Maximum Dosage. The sweeteners listed are sorbitol, mannitol, isomalt, maltitol, lactitol, xylitol, acesulfame K, aspartame, cyclamic acid and its Na and Ca salts, saccharin and its Na, K and Ca salts, thaumatin and neohesperdine DC. The Annex further provides extensive lists of the foodstuffs to which each sweetener can be added, with the maximum usable dose recorded in the right-hand column. When the maximum usable dose is recorded as *quantum satis,* sweeteners should be used in accordance with Good Manufacturing Practice, at a dose level not higher than is necessary to achieve the intended purpose. Where there is debate over whether an additive can be added to a particular category of foodstuff under the terms of the Directive, the matter can be referred by a representative of the Member State to the Standing Committee on Foodstuffs for its opinion and subsequently referred to the Commission for its resolution.

The presence of a sweetener within a foodstuff has to be labelled "with sweetener", as required by the framework Labelling Directive 2000/13/EC. The sales description of a table-top sweetener must include the name of the sweetening substance(s) used in its composition. Furthermore, table-top sweeteners containing polyols should include the warning "excessive consumption may induce laxative effects" and those containing aspartame the warning "contains a source of phenylalanine".

Finally, the Directive requires Member States to establish systems to monitor the consumption and use of sweeteners within 3 years of its coming into force and to report to the Commission within a further 2 years on the levels and use of sweeteners in foodstuffs.

9.1.3 Directive 94/36/EC of 30 June 1994 on colours for use in foodstuffs

This Directive regulates food colouring for similar reasons to those given in the recitals to its sister Directive on sweeteners. Of primary concern is the need to protect and inform the consumer. However, it also recognises the value of food colouring in:

- restoring the original appearance of food whose colour has been affected by processing, storage, packaging and distribution - making food more visually appealing;
- helping to identify flavours normally associated with particular foods;
- and reinforcing colours already present in food.

In essence, the colouring Directive prescribes in its Annexes the substances that can be used as colours in foodstuffs and the foodstuffs to which colours may be added. Colours are defined as:

- substances that add or restore colour in a food, and include natural constituents of foodstuffs and natural sources that are normally not consumed as foodstuffs as such and not normally used as characteristic ingredients of food; and
- preparations obtained from foodstuffs and other natural source materials obtained by physical and/or chemical extraction resulting in a selective extraction of the pigments relative to its nutritive or aromatic constituents.

However, the term does not include dried or concentrated foodstuffs used in the manufacture of compound foodstuffs because of their aromatic or nutritive properties, such as paprika, turmeric and saffron. Nor does it include colours used for the colouring of the inedible external parts of foodstuffs, such as cheese coatings and sausage casings.

Only the substances listed in Annex I may be used as colours in foodstuffs and sold directly to consumers, with the exception of E numbers E123, E127, E128, E154, E160b, E161g, E173 and E180[5]. Colours permitted for certain uses only are listed in Annex IV. Colours permitted in general foodstuffs are listed in Annex V. The maximum levels indicated in the Annexes relate to ready-to-eat foodstuffs prepared according to the instructions for use and to the quantities of colouring principle contained in the colouring preparation.

As with the sweeteners Directive, this Directive provides for a mechanism for resolving whether a substance is a colour within the meaning of the Directive, or whether a particular foodstuff belongs to a category of foods mentioned in the Annexes. Should, for example, a foodstuff manufacturer wish to add a substance to the list of approved colours, the representative of the relevant Member State should refer the matter to the Standing Committee on Foodstuffs for its opinion and subsequently to the Commission for its approval.

Finally, the Directive requires Member States to establish systems to monitor the consumption and use of colours within 3 years of its coming into force and to report to the Commission within a further 2 years on the levels and use of colouring in foodstuffs. A similar monitoring system is envisaged in the sweeteners Directive.

9.1.4 *Directive 95/2/EC of 20 February 1995 on food additives other than colours and sweeteners, as amended by Directives 96/85/EC, 98/72/EC, and 2001/5/EC*

The final component of the comprehensive Directive on additives, this Directive permits the use of additives other than sweeteners and colourings that are listed in its Annexes I, III, IV and V. It does not apply to enzymes (other than those mentioned in the Annexes). The use of the additives listed in the Annexes is limited to the following purposes: preservatives,

---

[5] The lists contained in the Annexes are extensive and can be downloaded from the Eur-Lex Web site at www.europa.eu.int/eur-lex.

antioxidants, carriers, acids, acidity regulators, anti-caking agents, anti-foaming agents, bulking agents, emulsifiers, emulsifying salts, firming agents, flavour enhancers, foaming agents, gelling agents, glazing agents, humectants, modified starches, packaging gases, propellants, raising agents, sequestrants, stabilisers, thickeners and flour treatment agents other than emulsifiers. However, the following are not considered as additives and are therefore not regulated by this Directive: substances used for the treatment of drinking water, products containing pectin and derived from apple pomace or peel of citrus fruits, chewing gum bases, white or yellow dextrin, roasted or dextrinated starch, ammonium chloride, blood plasma, edible gelatin, protein hydrolysates, milk protein and gluten, and amino acids, caseinates, casein and inulin.

Annex I lists all food additives that may be added to any foodstuff except: unprocessed foodstuffs, honey, non-emulsified oils and fats of animal or vegetable origin, butter, unflavoured, live fermented milk products, natural mineral water, coffee (excluding flavoured instant coffee), unflavoured leaf tea, sugars, dry pasta and natural unflavoured buttermilk. Annex II qualifies Annex I. It lists those foodstuffs in which only a limited number of the additives mentioned in Annex I may be used and prescribes maximum levels for their use. Annex III lists conditionally permitted preservatives and antioxidants, Annex IV other permitted additives, and Annex V permitted carriers and carrier solvents.

As with the previous Directives on food additives, this Directive contains similar provisions for adding substances to the lists in the Annexes and also requires Member States to set up monitoring systems for the use by consumers of additives permitted by this Directive.

9.2   Flavourings

There is not as yet in place a positive list of flavourings that are authorised for use within the EU. A Community-wide Register of flavourings that are sold and used in Member States is currently being evaluated by the Scientific Committee on Foods. EU legislation on flavourings is contained in a framework Directive and two Regulations.

9.2.1 Directive 88/388/EEC on the approximation of laws relating to flavourings for use in foodstuffs and to source materials for their production, as amended by Directive 91/71/EEC

The framework Directive on food flavouring lays down provisions on definitions of flavourings, general purity criteria, labelling, general rules for the use of flavourings within the internal market and maximum levels for substances that raise concern for human health. It does not lay down lists of approved flavourings, but makes provision for the Council of Ministers to adopt subsequent rules. Member States are required by the framework Directive to ensure that flavourings are not marketed or used on their territories unless they comply with this Directive.

The Directive applies to flavourings intended for use in or on foodstuffs to impart odour and/or taste, and to source materials used for the production of flavouring. Flavouring is defined[6] as meaning "flavouring substances, flavouring preparations, process flavourings, smoke flavourings or mixtures thereof". The term "flavouring substance" is limited to "a defined chemical substance"[7]. The Directive does not apply, therefore, to material of vegetable or animal origin, having inherent flavouring properties, where they are not used as flavouring sources, or to edible substances or substances that have an exclusive sweet, sour or salt taste.

Most significantly, Member States are required to take all necessary steps to ensure that flavourings do not contain any undesirable substance or other substance in a toxicologically dangerous quantity – substances that are naturally present in source materials for flavourings such as herbs may be harmful to human health in excessive quantities. Moreover, any substances that may have adverse effects on public health will only be approved after consulting the Scientific Committee for Food. Maximum limits for the use of certain flavourings are listed in Annexes I and II; these substances are: benzopyrene, agaric acid, aloin, β-asarone, berberine, coumarin,

---

[6] See Article 1(2)
[7] The limitation of this definition is addressed by the Commission in the White paper on Food Safety (paragraph 77).

hydrocyanic acid, hypericine, pulegone, quassine, safrole and isosafrole, santonin and thuyone.

The labelling rules for flavourings are set out in the framework Directive as superseded by the Labelling Directive 2000/13/EC. They apply to flavourings that are sold to both food producers and consumers. The word "flavouring" must be present in the ingredients list on the packaging of food products that contain flavouring. In addition, further labelling is required addressing minimum durability, conditions for storage and use, and identification of the manufacturer and of any other substances contained in the flavouring. The expression "natural flavouring" may be used only for flavouring substances or flavouring preparations that are extracted from vegetable or animal materials.

9.2.2   Regulation 2232/96/EC laying down a Community procedure for flavouring substances used or intended for use in or on foodstuffs

The framework Directive was followed by Regulation EC/2232/96, which lays down the procedure for establishing the authorisation of flavouring substances within the Community and creates at Commission level a Register of approved flavourings.

Under the terms of the Regulation, the general criteria for the authorisation of flavouring substances are twofold:

● that they present no risk to the health of the consumer in accordance with a scientific assessment carried out by the Scientific Committee for Food; and

● their use does not mislead the consumer.

The procedure for authorisation was as follows. Member States were required to notify the Commission within a year of the Regulation coming into force with a list of the flavouring substances that might, in accordance with the framework flavouring Directive (above), be used in foodstuffs marketed on their territory. Information on purity, chemical specification, natural occurrence in food, total amount added to foods and results of toxicological and metabolic studies was (and is) considered to be essential for evaluation of the substances at Community level. Such notifications were then scrutinised by the Commission Scientific Committee on Food before being entered in a Register of approved flavouring substances within the Community. The Register contains approximately 2,800 substances, adopted by Commission Decision 1999/217/EC and amended by Commission Decision 2000/489/EC. The Commission is currently carrying out a 5-year evaluation programme of the flavouring substances contained in the Register, some of which may be deleted if they do not meet the twofold criteria set out above, after the completion of which a Community-wide positive list of flavouring substances for use in foodstuffs shall be established. This is not expected until 2005 at the earliest[8].

Regulation 22332/96/EC makes further provision for amending the Register by adding further flavourings, and contains a safeguard clause that permits Member States temporarily to restrict the marketing of a flavouring on their territory on grounds of public health.

9.3   Conclusion

The system of approved lists introduced by the comprehensive Directive on additives and the framework Directive and Regulation on flavourings is considered to have achieved its objective in ensuring that the consumer is protected from additives and flavouring substances that might pose a risk to human health. It has also been successful in harmonising the approval of additives and flavouring within the internal market. Where it has been less effective is in keeping up with the pace of scientific and technological

---

[8] See Regulation 1565/2000/EC, which lays down the measures necessary for the adoption and evaluation programme in application of Regulation 2232/96/EC. The Regulation expedites the approval procedure of substances on the register and further provided that any person who wished to use a flavouring that was on the register but which had not yet been categorised by
- the Scientific Committee on Food in Category 1; or
- the Committee of Experts on Flavouring Substances of the Council of Europe (CEFS) in Category A; or
- the Joint FAO/WHO Expert Committee on Food Additives (JECFA)
had to provide the Commission with information for the evaluation of the substance within 12 months of the Regulation being adopted (July 2000).

developments – the procedure for amending the lists can take up to 2 or more years.

The White Paper on Food Safety highlights areas of additives and flavourings regulation in need of reform. Firstly it recommends that implementing powers should be conferred on the Commission to maintain the Community lists of authorised additives and that the status of enzymes should be clarified. Secondly, the Community lists of colouring matters, sweeteners and other additives need to be updated. Thirdly, the Commission recommends that the purity criteria for sweeteners, colours and other additives should be amended so that appropriate purity criteria for food additives made from novel sources can be laid down.

With regard to flavourings, the Commission comments that specific action has thus far concentrated on chemically defined substances. More work is needed to reflect innovation in this field and new insight into toxicological effects of substances naturally present in flavourings. The Commission has also undertaken to update the register of flavouring substances, establish a programme for their evaluation and lay down a list of additives authorised for use in flavourings.

Finally, the Commission published on 1 October 2001 a report on the "Dietary Food Additive Intake of the European Union"[9]. As mentioned above, the comprehensive Directive on additives required Member States to monitor the consumption and usage of food additives and submit a report to the Commission within three years of the coming into force of each Directive. In turn, the Commission was required to submit a report on this monitoring exercise to the European Parliament and Council. The report comments that, as a first attempt to obtain an overview of dietary food additive intake in the EU, the report has many limitations, not least of which was insufficient data and a failure by some Member States to use the same methodology. Nonetheless, the results obtained indicate, albeit on a preliminary basis, that the intake of the majority of food additives permitted

---

[9] This report, as with others, can be downloaded from the DG Sanco Web site (www.europa.eu.int/comm/foods).

today in the EU falls below the acceptable daily intake set by the Scientific Committee on Food. A further report will be produced within 3 years of the date of this report.

10. FOODS FOR PARTICULAR NUTRITIONAL USES AND FOOD SUPPLEMENTS

10.1 Introduction

"Foods for particular nutritional uses"[1], meaning dietary or dietetic foods, are foods that are produced to meet the specific requirements of the category of consumers for whom they are mainly intended. They are closely regulated within the European Union to ensure that human health is protected and that consumers are not, as is sometimes the case, misled.

"Food supplements" cover a wide range of products that have been marketed within the Community for a number of years without harmonisation under EU legislation. They are usually concentrated sources of nutrients or other substances (marketed in dose form) with a nutritional or physiological effect whose purpose is to supplement the intake of nutrients in the normal diet. In this field, the Commission has recently adopted a proposal for a Directive that would harmonise the substantially diverging national rules on the sale of food supplements containing minerals and vitamins. This proposal was adopted by the EU on 10 June 2002[2].

10.2 Foods for Particular Nutritional Uses

10.2.1 Framework Directive 89/398/EEC

10.2.1.1 Definitions

The framework Directive on foods intended for particular nutritional uses, as amended by Directives 96/84/EC and 1999/41/EC, regulates the composition, labelling and selling of dietetic foods. It defines foods for nutritional uses as foods that:

"owing to their special composition or manufacturing process are clearly distinguishable from foodstuffs for normal consumption,

---

[1] or "PARNUTs"

[2] Directive 2002/46/EC on the approximation of the laws of the Member States relating to food supplements

which are suitable for their claimed nutritional purposes and which are marketed in such a way as to indicate such suitability."

A particular nutritional use must fulfil the particular nutritional requirements:

i) of certain categories of persons whose digestive processes or metabolism are disturbed; or

ii) of certain categories of persons who are in a special physiological condition and who are therefore able to obtain special benefit from controlled consumption of certain substances in foodstuffs; or

iii) of infants and young children in good health."[3]

Foods falling within categories (i) or (ii) above are defined as "dietetic" or "dietary", and should be labelled accordingly.

10.2.1.2 Specific Directives

The framework Directive lists in its Annex the groups of foods for particular nutritional use to which subsequent and "specific" Directives should apply. There are currently in force four specific Directives on:

i) foods intended for use in energy-restricted diets for weight reduction;

ii) infant formulae and follow-on formulae;

iii) processed cereal-based foods and foods for infants and young children;

iv) foods for special medical purposes.

The specific Directives are considered below. The Annex also mentions specific Directives on foods "intended to meet the expenditure of intense muscular effort, especially for sportsmen", and foods for persons suffering from diabetes. With regard to the former category, the Commission

---

[3] Article 1

announced in its White Paper on Food Safety[4] that it intends shortly to propose a Directive regulating this increasingly important foodstuff; with regard to the latter category, the Commission has until 8 July 2002 to present a report to the other Community institutions on the desirability of adopting special provisions for foods for diabetics.

10.2.1.3 Requirements of framework Directive

It is important to note that the framework Directive does not prohibit selling foods for particular nutritional use that fall beyond the scope of the groups listed in the Annex (i.e. which are not regulated by the specific Directives) so long as they comply with the requirements of its provisions, particularly the labelling requirements. Accordingly, Member States are prohibited from restricting the free flow of these foodstuffs. This, however, is subject to the usual safeguard clause, which can be invoked by a Member State in cases of sudden risk to public health posed by foodstuffs regulated under either this framework Directive or the specific Directives.

Monitoring

The Directive imposes monitoring tasks on national food ("competent") authorities for dietary foods that are not governed by specific Community provisions. Whenever a manufacturer launches a new product it is required to notify the relevant national authority and submit a model of the label to be used. This applies equally to importers importing a product from a country outside the EU for the first time. Where the same product is subsequently placed on the market in a different Member State, the manufacturer, or, where appropriate, the importer, will also have to provide the same information to the relevant authority in that Member State. The relevant authority can further require the manufacturer/importer to produce the scientific work and data that establish that the foodstuff meets the definition of a food for particular nutritional purposes and complies with the labelling requirements. Such information as is gathered by national

---

[4] Paragraph 105, Ch 7

authorities should then regularly be passed on to the Commission. The Commission is required to report on the implementation of the monitoring duties of the Member States under this Directive by 8 July 2002 and every 3 years thereafter.

Labelling

The Labelling Directive (2000/13/EC)[5] applies to all foods for a particular nutritional use, but with the following further constraints imposed by this Directive:

● No foodstuffs other than those meeting the definition of "dietetic" or "dietary" can be so labelled, with the exception of foodstuffs for normal consumption that are authorised by the Standing Committee on Foodstuffs as suitable for a particular nutritional use.

● The designation under which a product is sold should be accompanied by an indication of its particular nutritional characteristics, or, in respect of foods for infants and young children, the purpose for which it is intended.

● The labelling of products under this Directive must also include:

i) the particular elements of the qualitative and quantitative composition or the special manufacturing process that gives the product its particular characteristics;

ii) the available energy value expressed in kilojoules ("kJ") and kilocalories ("kcal") and the carbohydrate, protein and fat content per 100 g or 100 ml of the product as marketed and, where appropriate, per specified quantity of the product as proposed for consumption;

---

[5] See Chapter 7

iii)   if, however, the energy value is less than 50 kilojoules per 100 g or 100 ml, these particulars may be replaced by the words "energy value less than 50 kilojoules per 100 grams/millilitres".

Finally, no claims as to the prevention, treatment or cure of human disease can be made on the labelling or packaging of foods for a particular nutritional purpose. This is a requirement of both this framework Directive and the Labelling Directive.

New product launching

An amendment to the Directive introduces the possibility of 2-year authorisations for foodstuffs for particular nutritional uses that do not meet all of the compositional rules as laid down in the specific Directives. This amendment was introduced to allow consumers to benefit more rapidly from scientific progress. In such circumstances, the Commission, on the application of a Member State, will consult the Scientific Committee for Food before deciding whether to authorise the food concerned for a period of 2 years. The Commission may also specify labelling requirements to be applied during the same period. Within the 2-year period, it is envisaged that the product will be able to be incorporated into one of the specific Directives.

Nutritional substances that can be added to foods for particular nutritional use

The framework Directive, as amended, requires the Commission to adopt a list of substances with specific nutritional purposes that can be added to foods for particular nutritional uses (unless otherwise provided for under a specific Directive) in order to ensure that the particular nutritional requirements of the persons for whom the foods are intended are fulfilled. The Annex to Directive 2000/15/EC on substances that may be added for specific nutritional purposes to foods for particular nutritional use accordingly lists the following categories as permissible substances:

vitamins, minerals, amino acids, carnitine and taurine, nucleotides, and choline and inositol.

10.2.1.4 Requirements of specific Directives

i)   *Directive 96/8/EC on foods intended for use in energy-restricted diets for weight reduction*

This specific Directive lays down compositional and labelling requirements for foods for particular nutritional uses intended for use in energy-restricted diets for weight reduction. For such foods to be marketed in the Community, they should comply with the terms of this Directive. Two distinct categories are foreseen:

i)   products presented as a replacement for the whole of the daily diet;

ii)   products presented as a replacement for one or more meals of the daily diet.

Composition

Weight-reducing foods for energy-restricted diets have to comply with the composition requirements listed in Annex I to the Directive. These prescribe maximum limits for the energy provided by a product, maximum protein content in terms of provision of energy, maximum fat content in terms of energy and the maximum dietary fibre content of the product. It also lists the vitamins and minerals to be used for each category of weight-reducing food. The nutritional substances that can be added to these foods to ensure that the particular nutritional requirements of the persons for whom the foods are intended are fulfilled are, as with the framework Directive, set out in Directive 2001/15/EC (above).

Packaging and labelling

All individual components making up the products presented as a replacement for the whole of the daily diet above should be contained in the same packaging.

The provisions of the framework labelling Directive 2000/13/EC apply to these foods, with the following further constraints:

- Products falling within category i) above shall be sold under the name: "Total diet replacement for weight control"; products falling within category ii) above shall be sold under the name "meal replacement for weight control".

- The particulars on the labelling should include:

    a) the available energy value and the content of proteins, carbohydrates and fat;

    b) the average quantity of each mineral and vitamin for which there are mandatory requirements stipulated in the Annex;

    c) instructions for appropriate preparation;

    d) where the food provides a daily intake of polyols in excess of 20 g, a statement to the effect that the food may have a laxative effect;

    e) a statement on the importance of maintaining an adequate daily fluid intake;

    f) for products presented as a replacement for the whole of the daily diet:

    –   a statement that the product provides adequate amounts of all essential nutrients every day;

    –   a statement that the product should not be used for more than 3 weeks without medical advice.

    g) for products presented as a replacement for one or more meals of the daily diet, a statement to the effect that the products are useful for the intended use only as part of an energy-restricted diet and that other foodstuffs should be a necessary part of such diet.

ii) *Directive 91/321/EEC on infant formulae and follow-on formulae, as amended by Directive 96/4/EC and 99/50/EC*

This specific Directive lays down compositional and labelling requirements for infant formulae and follow-on formulae. Infant formulae are foodstuffs that wholly satisfy the nutritional requirements for infants during the first 4 to 6 months of their life; as such, in order to safeguard their health, this Directive ensures that the only products suitable for such use are labelled "infant formulae". Follow-on formulae are foodstuffs intended for infants from the age of 4 months to 1 year that constitute the principal liquid element in a progressively diversified diet. Member States must ensure that products conforming to this Directive are allowed to be sold on their territories.

The Directive also requires Member States to give effect to the principles and aims of the International Code of Marketing of Breast-Milk Substitutes dealing with marketing, information and responsibilities of national health authorities in relation to these products.

Composition

Infant formulae must be manufactured from protein sources defined in the Annexes to the Directive and other food ingredients whose suitability for particular nutritional use by infants from birth has been established by generally accepted scientific data. The essential composition of such products is listed at Annex I of the Directive.

Follow-on formulae must be manufactured from protein sources that are defined in the Annexes to the Directive and other food ingredients whose suitability for particular nutritional use by infants from 4 months to 1 year has been established by generally accepted scientific data. The essential composition of such products is listed at Annex II.

The prohibition and limitations on the use of certain food ingredients are laid down in Annex I and II. In order to make the products ready for use, the Directive stipulates that nothing more than adding water should be required. Annex III lists the nutritional substances that can be added to these products. Pesticide residue limits of 0.01 milligram per kilogram of the product were set by an amendment to the Directive.

Labelling

The products should be sold under the names of "infant formula" and "product formula"; however, the selling names of products manufactured entirely from cows' milk proteins should be, respectively, "infant milk" and "follow-on milk". The obligations of the Labelling Directive will also apply to these foods. The following further particulars should also appear:

● In the case of infant formulae, a statement to the effect that the product is suitable for particular nutritional use by infants from birth when they are not breast-fed.

● In the case of infant formulae that do not contain added iron, a statement to the effect that, when the product is given to infants over 4 months, their total iron requirements must be met from additional sources.

● In the case of follow-on formulae, a statement to the effect that the product is suitable only for particular nutritional use by infants over the age of 4 months; that it should form only part of a diversified diet; and that it is not to be used as a substitute for breast-feeding during the first 4 months of life.

● In the case of both products:
  – the available energy value and the content of proteins, carbohydrates, and lipids;
  – the average quantity of each mineral and vitamin mentioned in Annex I and II, respectively; and
  – instructions for appropriate preparation of the product and a warning against the health hazards of inappropriate preparation.

● The labelling of both products should not discourage breast-feeding. The use therefore of the terms "humanised", "maternalised", or any such similar terms is not permitted. The labelling of infant formulae shall not include pictures of infants; nor shall it include other pictures or text that may idealise the use of the product.

● The labelling of infant formulae shall further contain the following:

‒ a statement concerning the superiority of breast feeding; and

‒ a statement recommending that the product should only be used on the advice of a medically qualified and independent person.

iii)   *Directive 96/5/EC on processed cereal-based foods and baby foods for infants and young children, as amended by Directive 98/36/EC and Directive 99/39/EC*

This specific Directive covers foodstuffs for particular nutritional use intended for use by infants (aged under 12 months) while they are being weaned and by young children (aged between 1 and 3 years) as a supplement to their diet and/or progressive adaptation to ordinary food. The foodstuffs shall comprise:

i)   processed cereal-based foods, which are divided into four categories:

‒ simple cereals that are or have to be reconstructed with milk or other liquids;

‒ cereals with an added high-protein food that have to be reconstructed with water or other protein-free liquid;

‒ pastas that are to be used after cooking in boiling water; and

‒ rusks and biscuits that are to be used either directly or, after pulverisation, with the addition of water, milk or other suitable liquids.

ii)   baby foods other than processed cereal-based foods.

The Directive does not apply to milks for young children. Member States should ensure that products falling within categories i) and ii) above are sold only in accordance with the requirements of this Directive.

Composition

Only ingredients whose suitability for use by infants and young children has been established by generally accepted scientific data should be used in the manufacture of these products. Annex I to the Directive lists the essential components together with minimum/maximum quantities of processed cereal-based foods for infants and young children. The list covers cereals, protein, carbohydrates, lipids and minerals. Annex II lists the essential components together with their minimum/maximum quantities of baby food for infants and young children. The list covers protein, carbohydrates, fat, sodium and vitamins.

Only the nutritional substances listed in Annex IV may be added in the manufacture of processed cereal-based foods and baby foods.

Specific rules on the presence of pesticides residues in these products are contained in Directive 99/39/EC. They require that baby food contains no detectable levels of pesticide residues, meaning no more than 0.01 milligram of pesticide residues per kilogram.

Labelling

The requirements of the Labelling Directive apply to these foods. The following further particulars should also appear:

● a statement as to the appropriate age from which the product may be used, being not less than 4 months;

● if the minimum age indicated is below 6 months, information as to the presence or absence of gluten;

- the available energy value, and the protein, carbohydrate and lipid content;

- instructions for appropriate preparation, and a statement of the importance of following those instructions.

iv)   Directive 1999/21/EC on dietary foods for special medical purposes

This, the final of the specific Directives, lays down compositional and labelling requirements for dietary foods for special medical purposes. These foods are intended to meet the specific nutritional requirements of persons suffering from medical conditions and are to be used under medical supervision. There are numerous examples of such foods, each manufactured to meet a very specific medical need, and it is an area characterised by rapid scientific innovation. As such, the Commission recognises through this Directive that it would be impossible to legislate for the composition of each individual product; instead, the Directive focuses on labelling and monitoring requirements for all foods for special medical purposes and prescribes maximum levels of vitamin and mineral substances for certain products. Only dietary foods for special medical purposes that comply with the terms of the Directive can be sold within the Community.

The Directive defines "dietary foods for special medical purposes" as "a category of foods for particular nutritional uses specially processed or formulated and intended for the dietary management of patients and to be used under medical supervision. They are intended for the exclusive or partial feeding of patients with a limited, impaired or disturbed capacity to take, digest, absorb, metabolise or excrete ordinary foodstuffs or certain nutrients contained therein or metabolites, or with other medically determined nutrient requirements, whose dietary management cannot be achieved only by modification of the normal diet, by other foods for particular nutritional uses, or by a combination of the two."

Such foods are classified into three categories:

i) nutritionally complete foods with a standard nutrient formulation that may constitute the sole source of nourishment for the intended recipient;

ii) nutritionally complete foods with a nutrient-adapted formulation specific for a disease, disorder or medical condition that may constitute the sole source of nourishment for the intended recipient;

iii) nutritionally incomplete foods with a standard formulation or a nutrient-adapted formulation specific for a disease, disorder or medical condition that are not suitable to be used as the sole source of nourishment.

Composition

The Directive establishes that dietary foods for special medical purposes should be based on sound medical and nutritional principles; i.e. their use must be safe, beneficial and effective in meeting the particular nutritional requirements of their recipients, as demonstrated by generally accepted scientific data. The Annex specifies the vitamins and minerals that should be used in foods for special medical purposes that are intended specifically for children under the age of 12 months and for foods falling within category (ii) above that are not intended for children under the age of 12 months.

Monitoring

Where a product falling under this Directive is placed on the market within the Community, the manufacturer or importer should inform the relevant national food authority by forwarding a model of the label to be used.

Labelling

The obligatory provisions of the Labelling Directive apply to these foods. The following further particulars should also appear:

● the name of the food will appear as: "Food(s) for special medical purposes".

- the available energy value, and the content of protein, carbohydrate and fat.

- the average quantity of each mineral substance and vitamin listed in the Annex.

- the following mandatory particulars, preceded by the words "important notice":

  - a statement that the product must be used under medical supervision;

  - a statement as to whether the product is suitable for use as the sole source of nourishment;

  - a statement indicating that the product is intended for a specific age group;

  - where appropriate, a statement that the product poses a health hazard if used by persons who are not suffering from the medical conditions for which it is intended.

- the statement "For the dietary management of [medical condition]".

- a description of the properties and/or characteristics that make the product useful particularly in relation to the nutrients that have been increased or reduced and the rationale for the use of the product.

10.3   Food Supplements

The Commission presented its proposal for a Directive on food supplements in May 2000 (COM(2000) 222 final, as amended by COM(2001) 159 final) in response to an increase in the use of pills and capsules as diet supplements and in response to inconsistent national rules on, and attitudes to, the proliferation of such products. Its aim is not to restrict, but to regulate, the sale of food supplements in the EU in the ultimate aim of protecting the consumer.

Food supplements are defined in the proposed Directive on food supplements as all foodstuffs that are concentrated sources of nutrients, alone or in combination, and marketed in dose form (i.e. pill, capsule, sachet, ampoule, etc.), whose purpose is to supplement the intake of those nutrients in the normal diet.

The objective of the Proposal is two-fold. Firstly, it establishes a general framework and safety rules for food supplements containing vitamins and minerals. (Other substances present in food supplements, such as fatty acids, fibres, plants, herbs and their extracts are not affected by this Directive.) The Proposal establishes lists of the vitamins and their forms that can be used in the manufacture of food supplements. It also stipulates that maximum limits for vitamin and mineral intake should be based on scientific risk assessment, on data on vitamin and mineral intake from other foods, and also on recommended daily doses of vitamins and minerals, all of which must be assessed by the Scientific Committee on Food. In due course, maximum units for vitamins and minerals in food supplements will be applied. Only vitamins and minerals authorised by the Scientific Committee for Food and listed in the Annexes to the Proposal are to be used in the manufacture of food supplements.

Secondly, it prescribes harmonised rules for the labelling of food supplements in order to ensure that consumers are in a position to make an informed choice. Labels will have to include clear instructions for daily dosage, a warning about possible health risk in case of excessive use, and a statement that the pills should not be used as a substitute for a varied diet. Claims that the product can prevent, treat or cure illness are prohibited, and any language suggesting that a varied diet does not provide the necessary amounts of essential nutrients is also prohibited.

On 27 September 2001, the Proposal was the subject of agreement within the European Council (The Internal Market, Tourism and Consumer Affairs Council) after a first reading in the European Parliament. The Council will in due course adopt a common position, which will in turn be communicated to the European Parliament for its second reading, following the course laid down by the co-decision procedure. It is intended that the Directive will enter into force on 31 May 2002, allowing the marketing of products that comply with the Directive from June 2002 and prohibiting the marketing of products that do not respect its rules by June 2004 at the latest. The Directive was finally adopted on 10 June 2002: Directive 2002/46/EC on the approximation of laws of the Member States relating to food supplements.

10.4   Conclusions

The primacy of food safety and the need for informed consumer choice, as outlined in the White Paper, will mean that the marketing of foodstuffs claiming to serve a particular need – an area of food production that is proliferating owing to consumer demand - will be increasingly supervised by the Commission. In this regard, a proposal on fortified foods (foods to which nutrients have been added) is expected from the Commission in 2002. In addition, the Commission is formulating a comprehensive policy on nutrition, which will be presented in the form of an Action Plan. Nutrition is now recognised as being one of the major determinants of human health; there are trends in the Member States, such as obesity, which have raised public health concerns and caused the Commission to consider that the promotion of a healthy diet is an increasingly important policy objective.

11. GENETICALLY MODIFIED ORGANISMS AND NOVEL FOODS

11.1   Introduction

There is no topic of European Union food law that has attracted more impassioned or polarised debate than the use of GMOs in food and animal feed.

A genetically modified organism is an organism "in which the genetic material has been altered in a way that does not occur naturally by mating and/or natural recombination"[1]. In agriculture, genetic modification has typically been used to modify commodity food crops such as corn and soya bean by introducing traits or combinations of traits that protect them from insects or provide tolerance to specific pesticides. Over 40 million hectares of land worldwide are currently used for the commercial production of GM crops, the United States, Canada and Argentina being the largest producers. The United States alone produces 70% of the world's GM crops. The main GM crops planted are soya bean (53% of global production), maize (27%), cotton (9%) and oilseeds (8%)[2]. The EU, by contrast, farms less than 20,000 hectares of GM crops (0.03% of the world total), most of which is maize.

11.2   Directive 90/220/EEC on the Deliberate Release into the Environment of GMOs

In the late 80s, the Commission proposed a Directive to harmonise the authorisation procedure for the deliberate release of GMOs into the environment (under Part B of the Directive) and the selling of products containing, or consisting of, GMOs (under Part C of the Directive). It was intended to regulate, therefore, both the production of GM crops and the sale of GM products. Articles 10-18 of Directive 90/220/EEC, which make up Part C, laid down a Community procedure permitting national food authorities to consent to such products being sold on their territory, subject

---

[1] See Article 2 of Directive 200/18/EC
[2] Figures taken from the Commission's "Consumer Voice", Special Edition, September 2001s

to the Commission's approval and an absence of objections from other Member States[3]. Underpinning the system of authorisation was the need for the environmental risk assessment undertaken by the national food authority and reviewed by the Commission and other Member States to show that the genetic modification was not liable to result in any toxic or other harmful effects for human health or the environment[4]. Importantly (in light of subsequent consumer reaction) the Directive did not require all GM products to be compulsorily labelled so as to enable the ultimate consumer fully to exercise his or her freedom of choice over purchasing GM foods. It was not until Regulation 258/97/EC on novel foods came into force that obligatory labelling was required for GM products.

Eighteen GMOs have been authorised under Directive 90/220/EEC. They are as follows[5]:

Product	Notifier	Date of Commission decision
Vaccine against Aujesky's disease	Vemie Veterinar Chemie GmbH	18.12.92
Vaccine against rabies	Rhone-Merieux	19.10.93
Tobacco tolerant to bromoxynil	SEITA	08.06.94
Vaccine against Aujesky's disease (further uses)	Vemie Veterinar Chemie GmbH	18.07.94

---

[3] In *Association Greenpeace France and Others v Ministère de l'Agriculture et de la Pêche and Others*, with Monsanto Europe and Novartis Seeds intervening as third parties, it was held by the ECJ that, once the Commission had approved the authorisation of a GM product, the "competent" authority that had forwarded the application with, needless to say, a favourable opinion, was obliged to consent to the product being sold on its territory. This decision will pertain equally to the authorisation procedure incorporated in the new GMO Directive 2001/18/EC, which comes into force in October 2002.
[4] But see Article 9 of the novel food Regulation, which now applies to authorisations under Part C
[5] Both tables that follow are updated on DG SANCO's Web site under "GMOs"

Product	Notifier	Date of Commission decision
Male sterile swede rape resistant to glufosinate ammonium (MS1, RF1). Uses: breeding activities	Plant Genetic Systems	06.02.96
Soya beans tolerant to glyphosate Uses: import and processing	Monsanto	03.04.96
Male sterile chicory tolerant to glufosinate ammonium. Uses: breeding activities	Bejo-Zaden BV	20.05.96
Bt-maize tolerant to glufosinate ammonium (Bt-176)	Ciba-Geigy	23.01.97
Male sterile swede rape tolerant to glufosinate ammonium (MS1 RF1) (further uses)	Plant Genetic Systems	06.06.97
Male sterile swede rape tolerant to glufosinate ammonium (MS1 RF2)	Plant Genetic Systems	06.06.97
Test kit to detect antibiotic residues in milk	Valio Oy	14.07.97
Carnation lines with modified flower colour	Florigene	01.12.97
Swede rape tolerant to glufosinate ammonium (Topas 19/2). Uses: import and processing	AgrEvo	22.04.98
Maize tolerant to glufosinate ammonium (T25)	AgrEvo	22.04.98
Maize expressing the Bt crylA(b) gene (MON 810)	Monsanto	22.04.98
Maize tolerant to glufosinate ammonium and expressing the Bt crylA(b) gene (Bt-11) Uses: import and processing	Novartis	22.04.98
Carnation lines with improved vase life	Florigene	20.10.98
Carnation lines with modified flower colour	Florigene	20.10.98

For reasons that will be considered in due course, no further authorisations have been granted under the Directive since October 1998, although 12 are still pending. On 17 October 2002, the Directive will be repealed and replaced by the new GMO Directive 2001/18/EC, by which date the provisions of the new GMO Directive must be transposed into the domestic law of the Member States. The 12 pending applications are as follows:

Product notification details	Company
Maize expressing the Bt *cryIA(b)* gene (MON 809). Received by the Commission from France on 06.08.96. Favourable opinion of the EU Scientific Committee 19.05.98. Uses: as any other maize	Pioneer
Male sterile chicory[6]. Received by the Commission from the Netherlands on 20.09.96. Favourable opinion of the EU Scientific Committee 18.12.98. Uses: food and feed	Bejo-Zaden BV
Swede rape tolerant to glufosinate ammonium (FALCON GS40/90) Received by the Commission from Germany on 25.11.96. Uses: as any other swede rape	AgroEvo GmbH
Male sterile swede rape tolerant to glufosinate ammonium (MS8, RF3) Received by the Commission from Belgium on 16.01.97. Favourable opinion of the EU Scientific Committee 19.05.98. Uses: as any other swede rape	Plant Genetic Systems
Fodder beet tolerant to glyphosate Received by the Commission from Denmark on 19.10.97. Favourable opinion of the EU Scientific Committee 23.06.98	DLF-Trifolium, Monsanto and Danisco Seed
Cotton expressing the Bt *cryIA (c)* gene (line 531) Received by the Commission from Spain on 24.11.97. Favourable opinion of the EU Scientific Committee 14.07.98. Uses: as any other cotton	Monsanto

---

[6] This is the same product as no. 7 on the list of approved GMOs, which was restricted to breeding activities

149

GMOs and Novel Foods

Product notification details   Company

Cotton tolerant to herbicide (line 1445)   Monsanto
Received by the Commission from Spain on 24.11.97.
Favourable opinion of the EU Scientific Committee 14.07.98.
Uses: as any other cotton

Potato with altered starch composition   AMYLOGENE
Received by the Commission from Sweden on 20.05.98.
Uses: as any other starch potato

Swede rape tolerant to glufosinate ammonium (Liberator)   AgroEvo GmbH
Received by the Commission from Germany on 29.10.98.
Favourable opinion of the EU Scientific Committee 30.11.00
Uses: as any other swede rape

Maize tolerant to glufosinate ammonium and expressing the   Novartis
Bt *crylA(b)* gene (Bt-11)[7]
Received by the Commission from France and Spain on
12.04.99 and 03.05.99, respectively. 30.11.00 Favourable
opinion of the EU Scientific Committee Uses: cultivation

Maize tolerant to glufosinate ammonium and expressing the   Pioneer
Bt *crylA(b)* gene (T25 + MON810)[8]
Received by the Commission from the Netherlands on
29.04.99. Favourable opinion of the EU Scientific
Committee 06.06.00

Maize tolerant to glyphosate (GA21)   Monsanto
Received by the Commission from Spain on 20.05.99.
Favourable opinion of the EU Scientific Committee 22.09.00
Uses: as any other maize

---

[7] This is the same as no. 16 on the list of approved GMOs, which was restricted to import and processing
[8] This product is obtained from conventionally derived crosses between no.s 14 and 15 on the list of approved GMOs.

150

11.3   Paralysis in the Authorisation Process

Directive 90/220/EEC appeared on its face to be an effective means of implementing the EU's policy of allowing GMOs to be grown and used in food and feed products within the Community so long as they were considered safe; but what the legislators could not have foreseen was the extreme reaction that greeted the launch of GMOs and GM foods in certain Member States. Many consumers, supported by the clamorous campaigning of environmental non-governmental organisations, were not persuaded of the need or of the safety of this form of food production. Whereas in the United States there had been little consumer opposition to the launch of GMOs, in the European Union – a patchwork of Member States with a striking variety of different culinary cultures – a similarly consistent approach from consumers proved a vain hope. The debate, fuelled more by ethical and at times irrational fears than by robust scientific argument, had wider political ramifications for the EU. Governments of certain Member States did not want to jeopardise their positions by ignoring the clear – albeit at times populist - opposition to this form of biotechnology demonstrated by their citizens, and so refused to authorise GM products. The United States and other large GMO exporters in turn interpreted the failure to approve authorisations, in violation of requirements of EU law, as maladministration or, worse still, latent protectionism on behalf of the EU.

In October 1998, Denmark, France, Italy, Austria and Luxembourg, as a consequence of adverse consumer reaction to the marketing of GMOs in their respective countries, managed to push through the Council of Ministers a *de facto* moratorium on the authorisation of any new GMOs in the EU until safer procedures were put in place. The safer procedures envisaged were a more stringent and transparent regulatory framework for authorisations and a compulsory labelling and traceability régime. The moratorium is still in effect at the time of writing. Not only does it represent a direct challenge to the binding obligations that EU law places on Member States (in the form of Directive 90/220/EEC), it has effectively frozen any further development in this area of biotechnology, which is considered by many in the industry, and seemingly within the Commission, to present a crucial opportunity for innovation in food production. The Commission has been trying to resolve the impasse ever since. It has approached this task by proposing the following:

● replacing the existing GMO Directive with a stricter and more transparent regulatory framework in the form of Directive 2001/18/EC, which comes into force in October 2002;

● adopting two proposals for Regulations on the traceability and labelling of GMOs and GMO-derived products and further streamlining their authorisation procedure. (These proposals will not come into force before 2004.)

11.4 Directive 2001/18/EC on the Deliberate Release into the Environment of GMOs (and Repealing Directive 90/220/EEC)

This Directive introduces the following reforms to the regulation of GMOs in the EU:-

a) A more thorough risk assessment will take place prior to authorisation. This will include any long-term effects from interaction between GM crops and the natural environment. The "principles for the environmental risk assessment" are set out in Annex II. Part B of the Directive sets out the requirements for "deliberate release of GMOs for any other purpose than for placing on the market" and Part C the requirements for "placing on the market of GMOs as or in products". More particularly:

– Member States are required to ensure that GMOs that contain genes expressing resistance to antibiotics in use for medical or veterinary treatment are taken into particular consideration when carrying out an environmental risk assessment, with a view to identifying and phasing out antibiotic resistance markers in GMOs that may have adverse effects on human health and the environment. This phasing out should take place by

31 December 2008 for Part B authorisations, and by 31 December 2004 in the case of Part C authorisations.

- Member Sates must ensure that potential adverse effects on human health and the environment, which may occur directly or indirectly through gene transfer from GMOs to other organisms, are accurately assessed on a case-by-case basis. The assessment should be conducted in accordance with Annex II of the Directive and should take into account the long-term environmental impact in terms of both the nature of the organism being introduced and the receiving environment. Annex III lists information that will be required in the notification to the European Food Safety Authority. Annex III (A) (III) lists information that is required to meet "the conditions of release and the receiving environment". These include, *inter alia*, the quantities of GMOs to be released, post-release treatment of the site, proximity to drinking water supplies, and geographical traits of the area of release. Annex III (A) (IV) lists information required "relating to the interaction between the GMOs and the environment". These include, *inter alia*, predicted habitats of the GMOs, studies of the behaviour of GMOs and their ecological impact carried out in simulated natural environments (such as microcosms, growth rooms and greenhouses) and the genetic transfer capacity of the GMOs.

b) There will be a validity limit of 10 years on all authorisations for the marketing of GM products. Authorisation will be renewable for further 10-year periods.

c) As regards Part C authorisations, there will be ongoing monitoring of potential hazards so that preventive steps can be taken. Member States are required to ensure that their competent authorities organise inspections and other control measures as appropriate and that the producers of the GMOs comply with a "monitoring plan", the requirements of which are set out in Annex VII to the Directive. The objective of a monitoring plan is to:

- confirm that any assumption regarding the occurrence and impact of potential adverse effects of the GMO or its use are correct; and

- identify the occurrence of adverse effects of the GMO or its use on human health or the environment that were not anticipated.

d) The "precautionary principle" will be applied for the benefit of the environment and consumers. The Directive requires Member States, "in accordance with the precautionary principle, to ensure that all appropriate measures are taken to avoid adverse effects on human health and the environment which might arise from the deliberate release or the placing on the market of GMOs."[9] In practice, the precautionary principle will be applied where an unacceptable risk to health has been identified but further scientific information is needed to arrive at a more complete assessment of the risk[10].

e) There will be a procedure for regularly informing and updating EU citizens on GMO developments in Member States. Upon receipt of a notification for the marketing of a GMO or GM product, the European Food Safety Authority must immediately make available to the public the summary of the dossier provided by the competent authority that contains the required information concerning the organism and the reasoned scientific grounds for its authorisation. The competent authority's assessment report should also be made available. Any comments made by members of the public will then be relayed back to the competent authority. Furthermore, Member States and the European Food Safety Authority shall make available to the public information on all Part B releases of GMOs in their territory.

f) The labelling of GMOs or GM products marketed under Part C will be compulsory. Annex IV sets out in detail the information that will be required. On the label must be included the commercial name of the product, a statement that "This product contains genetically modified

---

[9] See Article 4 and the Commission's Communication on the precautionary principle COM (2000) 1
[10] See chapter 5 for further consideration of the precautionary principle

organisms", and the details of how to obtain further information. More detailed provisions on labelling (and traceability) are set out in the Commission proposals on GM food and feed (COM (2001) 425 and 182 final), which are considered below.

g) The European Food Safety Authority will become responsible for reviewing the risk assessment of all notifications under this Directive.

h) Existing consents granted under Directive 90/220/EEC will have to be renewed in order to avoid disparities with consents granted under the new Directive, and in order to comply with the more detailed pre-conditions for consent under this Directive. They will continue to remain in force but it will be necessary for the notifying companies to provide additional information concerning the risk assessment, methods for sampling and detection to the European Food Safety Authority within 6 months of the entry into force of Directive 2001/18/EC.

11.5   Commission Proposals for a Regulation on GM Food and Feed (COM(2001) 425 final) and for a Regulation Concerning Traceability and Labelling of Food and Feed Products Produced from GMOs (COM(2001) 182 Final)

To meet further consumer concerns, the Commission adopted two proposals on 25 July 2001, which together cover traceability, labelling, and a single, science-based and predictable authorisation process for GM food and feed. They were jointly drafted by DG for Health and Consumer Protection (DG SANCO) and DG Environment.

The first proposal (COM(2001) 425) concerns food and feed containing, consisting of, or produced from GMOs, as well as food and feed ingredients, including additives and flavourings, when they have been produced from GMOs. The proposal provides:

● a refined procedure for safety assessment of GM food;

- a safety assessment and an authorisation procedure for GM feed, based on the procedure used for GM food;

- that authorisation should not be granted for a single use either as food or feed where such products are likely to be used as both. Such products would therefore have to fulfil the authorisation criteria for both food and feed before being placed on the market (the Commission refers to this reform as "One door – one key");

- harmonised and comprehensive labelling requirements for GM products with the aim of providing the consumer "with a real choice"[11]. An appropriate labelling system is rightly regarded by the Commission as one of the key issues in ensuring greater acceptance of the application of gene technology in the food sector. The current labelling provisions will therefore be extended to all GM foods and feed. Food and food ingredients that contain or consist of GMOs will have to labelled as such, and even food and food ingredients produced from a GMO will have to be labelled as "produced from genetically modified [name of organism] but not containing a genetically modified organism".

The second of the two proposals (COM 2001(182)) will ensure that GMOs are labelled and traceable at every stage of production, manufacture and distribution of the food – in other words, from the "farm to the table". The obligation of traceability is intended:

- to permit accurate labelling of the final product;

- to provide means for inspection and control of labelling claims;

- to give the consumer the ultimate choice of whether to purchase a GM product; and

- to facilitate the rapid withdrawal of a product should an unforeseen risk to human health or the environment arise.

---

[11] See explanatory memorandum to the Proposal

The proposal's requirements for traceability largely build on the general requirements in the General Food Law Regulation12, which establishes the principle of traceability at all stages of the production and distribution chain in the food and feed sectors.

Labelling of GM feed will follow the same basic "farm to table" principles, thereby, for example, providing livestock farmers with accurate information on the composition and properties of feed.

11.6   Regulation 258/97/EC on Novel Foods and Novel Food Ingredients

This Regulation was enacted in order to ensure the free movement of trade in "novel foods and ingredients" and to establish a single safety assessment procedure for their use in the Community[13]. It also lays down compulsory labelling requirements. It should be noted, however, that the Commission Proposals (above) on GM food and feed will substantially amend this Regulation.

The Regulation applies to the placing on the market of novel foods and ingredients that have not before been used for human consumption within the Community and which fall under the following categories:

a)   foods and food ingredients containing or consisting of GMOs;

b)   foods and food ingredients produced from, but not containing, GMOs;

c)   food and food ingredients with a new or intentionally modified primary molecular structure;

d)   food and food ingredients consisting of or isolated from micro-organisms, fungi or algae;

---

[12] See Chapter 5

[13] The definition of novel foods and ingredients in this Regulation includes GM foods as regulated by the 1990 GMO Directive, but not GM feeds.

e) food and food ingredients consisting of or isolated from plants and food ingredients isolated from animals, except for foods and food ingredients obtained by traditional propagating or breeding practices and having a history of safe food use;

f) foods and food ingredients to which has been applied a production process not currently used, where that process gives rise to significant changes in the composition or structure of the foods or food ingredients that affect their nutritional value, metabolism or level of undesirable substances.

Foods falling within the above categories should not, under the terms of Article 3 of the Directive:

- present a danger for the consumer;
- mislead the consumer;
- differ from foods or food ingredients that they are intended to replace to such an extent that their normal consumption would be nutritionally disadvantageous for the consumer.

11.6.1 Authorisation procedure

An authorisation procedure for such foods is set out in Articles 4, 6, 7 and 8 of the Regulation. The manufacturer or retailer of a novel food is required to submit a request for authorisation to the Member State in which the food is to be sold and a copy request to the Commission[14]. The copy request to the Commission is, as with the GMO Directive, circulated for the attention of all other Member States. The request should contain a copy of the scientific studies that demonstrate that the product complies with the criteria laid down in Article 3. The competent authority of the Member State will then prepare an initial assessment, which in turn is forwarded to the

---

[14] Regulation 1852/2001/EC protects certain commercially confidential information provided to an authority under the novel foods regulation.

Commission and all other Member States for their comments and/or objections. If the competent authority considers that an additional assessment is required, or if another Member State objects to the marketing of the novel food, an authorisation decision will be taken by the Commission following an opinion from the Standing Committee for Foodstuffs.

This procedure applies to any food or food ingredient consisting of GMOs within the meaning of Directive 90/220/EEC[15] and so should be used instead of the procedure set out in Part C of the 1990 Directive. In the case of foods and food ingredients produced from, but not containing GMOs (which are not regulated by Directive 90/220/EEC) the novel foods Regulation also applies. However, no products consisting of or containing live GMOs have so far been marketed under this Regulation because of the moratorium. Recent approvals include "phospholipids from egg yolk"[16], pasteurised fruit-based preparations produced using high-pressure pasteurization,[17] and trehalose[18].

An exception to the requirement to comply with the above authorisation procedure applies to novel foods and ingredients falling within categories (b), (d) and (e) in paragraph 11.6 above, which "on the basis of the scientific evidence available and generally recognised or on the basis of an opinion delivered by one of the competent [authorities of the Member States], are substantially equivalent to existing foods or food ingredients as regards their composition, nutritional value, metabolism, intended use and the level of undesirable substances contained therein"[19]. If the competent authority considers that a product meets the test of "substantial equivalence", woolly though it is, it is permitted to authorise its sale without the need of the Commission's or other Member State's prior consent. There are currently 11 applications concerning GM products pending under this

[15] See Article 9
[16] Commission Decision 2000/195/EC
[17] Commission Decision 2001/424/EC
[18] Commission Decision 2001/721/EC
[19] See Article 5

exception; they include: processed oil from GM canola seed, processed oils (six varieties) from GM oilseed rape, and food and food ingredients produced from GM maize. Again, these too are in suspended animation awaiting a resolution of the moratorium.

11.6.2   Labelling requirements

One of the legislative purposes behind the adoption of the novel foods Regulation was to ensure that categories of novel foods and ingredients (including GMOs) were labelled so that the final consumer could be informed of the composition and nutritional value of the food. This was partly to fill the gap exposed by the 1990 GMO Directive, which did not require compulsory labelling. Accordingly, Article 8 lays down the detailed requirements for labelling of such products and leaves the implementation of the rules to be adopted by the Commission after consultation with the Standing Committee for Foodstuffs. Surprisingly, no rules have as yet been adopted. This unsatisfactory position was partially rectified by Regulation 1139/98/EC on GM soya and maize, which requires ingredients produced from GM maize and soya to be labelled, and will be wholly rectified by the Commission's two recent proposals. Additionally, GM additives and flavourings have to be labelled in accordance with Regulation 50/2000/EC on the labelling of foodstuffs and ingredients containing additives and flavourings.

11.7   Conclusion

The advent of biotechnology in food production has tested the regulatory capacity of the Commission to its limit and shown its limitations. In the face of widespread consumer mistrust of this form of gene technology, exacerbated as it is by repeated food scares, the Commission has been unable to allay the fears of either GM food producers on one side of the spectrum or consumers on the other. Any attempt by the Commission to recommence authorisations before the new legislation has come into effect have met with opposition, most recently in the Council of Ministers (Environment) in October 2001 – moreover, France, Italy and Greece have already indicated that they will not comply with Directive 2001/18/EC until the rules on traceability and labelling come into force, which is not expected until 2004. Other Member States demand that there should be clearly set out in the form of a further proposal the environmental responsibility and legal liability that will apply to producers of GM crops that harm the environment and its biodiversity. The question remains whether the Commission will allow these objections to continue to delay harmonised trade in safe GM foods within the Community.

12. INTERNATIONAL TRADE IN FOOD

12.1 Introduction

A harmonised system of international trade in food, where products are of similarly acceptable quality, is the ultimate aim of regulation in this field: universally uniform food standards not only bring down the cost to the consumer but also facilitate consumer protection. But this is very much an ideal; in practice, it has proved difficult to achieve.

This chapter will first consider the basic principles that govern international food trade. Much international trade in food is governed by international agreements and standards, although similar food safety principles usually underpin both intra-Community trade and trade with external ("third") countries. It will then consider the roles of the World Trade Organisation (WTO) and its Agreements, of the Codex Alimentarius, and of the WTO dispute settlement procedure, before concentrating on the EU-US hormone-treated beef dispute as an example of the difficulty with which trade disputes based on differing scientific opinion are resolved.

12.2 General Principles

A test of "equivalence" is generally applied to imports into the Community from third countries unless specific agreements[1] indicate otherwise. Imported food should comply with EU food law or equivalent regulation in force in the exporting country (see overleaf). Food exported from the Community should also comply with EU food law unless a specific agreement indicates otherwise or unless the importing country consents to the importation of food that does not meet Community standards (see overleaf). In addition, countries are encouraged to develop international technical standards as a means of achieving consistency in international trade. Where international standards exist, they should be taken into consideration in the development of food law.

---

[1] The Commission negotiates bilateral agreements on behalf of the EU

These principles have recently been enshrined in statute by the General Food Law Regulation. They merit setting out in full[2].

Article 11 provides:

Food and feed imported into the Community

"Food and feed imported into the Community for placing on the market within the Community shall comply with the relevant requirements of food law or conditions recognized by the Community to be at least equivalent thereto or, where a specific agreement exists between the Community and the exporting country, with requirements contained therein."

Article 12 provides:

Food and feed exported from the Community

"1. Food and feed exported or re-exported from the Community for placing on the market of a third country shall comply with the relevant requirements of food law, unless otherwise requested by the authorities of the importing country or established by the laws, regulations, standards, codes of practice and other legal and administrative procedures as may be in force in the importing country.

In other circumstances, except in the case where foods are injurious to health or feeds are unsafe, food and feed can only be exported or re-exported if the competent authorities of the country of destination have expressly agreed, after having been fully informed of the reasons for which and the circumstances in which the food or feed concerned could not be placed on the market in the Community.

---

[2] 178/2002/EC - see Chapter 5

2. Where provisions of a bilateral agreement concluded between the Community or one of its Member States and a third country are applicable, food and feed exported from the Community or that Member State to that third country shall comply with the said provisions."

Article 13 provides:

International standards
"Without prejudice to their rights and obligations, the Community and the Member States shall:

(a) contribute to the development of international technical standards for food and feed and sanitary and phytosanitary standards;

(b) promote the coordination of work on food and feed standards undertaken by international governmental and non-governmental organizations;

(c) contribute, where relevant and appropriate, to the development of agreements on recognition of the equivalence of specific food and food-related measures;

(d) give particular attention to the special development, financial and trade needs of developing countries, with a view to ensuring that international standards do not create unnecessary obstacles to exports from developing countries;

(e) promote consistency between international technical standards and food law while ensuring that the high level of protection adopted in the Community is not reduced."

12.3   World Trade Organisation (WTO)

The food safety implications of the international trade in foods are principally regulated by the WTO, which was established in 1995 after the conclusion of the Uruguay Round of the General Agreement on Tariffs and

Trade (GATT) negotiations, and now has 144 member countries. The European Commission represents the interests of the Member States in the WTO. The WTO oversees the operation of a rules-based, multilateral trading system between its members, and is responsible for the further liberalising of trade, for serving as a forum for future multilateral trade negotiations, and for acting as a Dispute Settlement Body (DSB) with jurisdiction over the full range of trade issues covered by the WTO sectoral agreements. These agreements have been described by the WTO as "legal ground-rules for international commerce"; essentially, they operate as contracts, guaranteeing member countries important trade rights and binding governments to keep to agreed trade policies. Members of the WTO are signatories to these agreements; two are of particular importance to food law.

The Uruguay Round of GATT incorporated for the first time within the multilateral trading system binding agreements on food safety. Participants at the Round recognised that measures ostensibly adopted by national governments to protect the health of their consumers could as easily be disguised as protectionist measures to prohibit imports. Consequently, the Technical Barriers to Trade Agreement and the Sanitary and Phytosanitary Measures Agreement (see further below) were included among the agreements annexed to the 1994 Marakesh Agreement, which established the WTO. All members of the WTO have agreed to abide by their terms. As a general principle of these agreements, the EU, along with other members of the WTO, is required to base any prohibition of the import of foodstuffs on international standards, or, in so far as they are not based on international standards, on measures that are scientifically warranted through appropriate risk assessment procedures.

12.3.1 Agreement on Technical Barriers to Trade (TBT)

This Agreement seeks to ensure that technical negotiations and standards (including packaging, marking and labelling requirements), as well as testing and certificate procedures, do not create unnecessary obstacles to trade; but it also recognises that countries have the right to establish protection at levels they consider appropriate - for example, for human, animal or plant life or health or environment, and should not be prevented from taking necessary measures to ensure that those levels of protection are met. The agreement therefore encourages countries to use international standards where appropriate, but it does not require them to change their levels of protection as a result of standardisation. Article 2.6 of the TBT Agreement states:

> "With a view to harmonising technical regulations on as wide a basis as possible, Members shall play a full part, within the limits of their resources, in the preparation by appropriate international standardising bodies of international standards for products for which they either adopted, or expect to adopt, technical regulations."

A Code of Good Practice for the Preparation, Adoption and Application of Standards is included as annex to the Agreement.

12.3.2   *Agreement on the Application of Sanitary and Phytosanitary Measures (SPS)*

This Agreement concerns the application of food safety, animal and plant health standards in international trade (*"phyto"* denotes "plant") and is of particular relevance to food law. The Agreement recognises that governments have the right to take SPS measures but stipulates that they should be applied only to the extent necessary to protect human, animal or plant life or health and should not arbitrarily or unjustifiably discriminate between member countries where identical or similar conditions prevail.

In order to harmonise SPS regulation on as wide a basis as possible, WTO members are encouraged to base their measures on international standards, guidelines and recommendations wherever they exist. Article 3.1 of the SPS Agreement states:

"To harmonise sanitary and phytosanitary measures on as wide a basis as possible, Members shall base their sanitary and phytosanitary measures on international standards, guidelines or recommendations, where they exist, except as otherwise provided for in this Agreement."

However, members may maintain or introduce measures that result in higher standards if scientifically justified or as a consequence of risk decisions based on an appropriate risk assessment. The Agreement then sets out the procedures and criteria for the assessment of risk and the determination of appropriate levels of SPS protection.

Members are expected to accept the SPS measures of others as being equivalent if the exporting country demonstrates to the importing country that its measures achieve the importing country's own level of health protection. Accordingly, the Agreement provides the right to obtain the risk assessment on which another country's measure is based.

The EU plays an active role in the SPS Committee, as with other WTO Committees, to ensure that the international framework defends the right of the EU Member States to maintain high public health standards for food safety. In this context, the EU has adopted a Communication on the precautionary principle[3] and is seeking to clarify within the existing WTO framework an agreement for its use in the international context.

12.4 Codex Alimentarius[4]

The Codex Alimentarius Commission was set up in 1963 as a joint instrument of the United Nations Food and Agriculture Organization (FAO) and the World Health Organization (WHO) to provide a forum in which food standards could be examined. Its primary purpose is to protect the health of consumers and ensure fair prices in the international trade in food. In this regard, the Codex Alimentarius ("the food code") formulates food

---

[3] COM (2000) 1
[4] The Web site for the Codex Alimentarius Commission can be found at www.fao.org

safety standards that serve as international guidelines for national governments and food business operators. Thus far it has adopted standards for commodities; codes of practice and maximum limits for additives, contaminants, pesticides residues and veterinary drugs; methods of sampling; and codes and guidelines of hygienic practice. Whilst Codex standards are not mandatory, they are influential in that products complying with Codex standards may be accepted or given free entry into the markets of other countries that are members of the Codex. Member States of the EU are members of the Codex Alimentarius. The EU is an observer to the Codex (in the form of the Commission, which represents the EU in international organisations) but is currently seeking to accede to the Codex Alimentarius.

The Codex guidelines have been adopted by the TBT Agreement and the SPS Agreement as being the relevant applicable standards. The adoption of Codex standards as scientifically justified norms for the purpose of these agreements is significant; by their adoption they have become an integral part of the legal framework within which international food trade is conducted and have already been used as a benchmark in international food trade disputes.

Additionally, the Codex has published the "Code of Ethics for International Trade in Food", the principal objective of which is to stop exporting countries and exporters from dumping poor-quality or unsafe food onto international markets. Although only a voluntary Code, it is worth setting out in full as its general principles will be persuasive in the context of a trade dispute:

"4.1 International trade in food should be conducted on the principle that all consumers are entitled to safe, sound and wholesome food and to protection from unfair trade practices."

4.2 No food should be in international trade which:

(a) has in it or upon it any substance in an amount which renders it poisonous, harmful or otherwise injurious to health; or

(b) consists in whole or in part of any filthy, putrid, rotten, decomposed or diseased substance or foreign matter, or is otherwise unfit for human consumption, or

(c) is adulterated; or

(d) is labelled, or presented in a manner that is false, misleading or is deceptive; or

(e) is sold, prepared, packaged, stored or transported for sale under insanitary conditions."

12.5   WTO Dispute Resolution Procedures

12.5.1   Dispute Settlement Understanding

The WTO dispute settlement system is one of the cornerstones of the multilateral trade order. It provides the machinery for mediation and resolution of trade disputes between WTO members under the WTO agreements and is responsible for enforcing the rule of law in a rules-based system of multilateral trade. (This, at any rate, is the intention; the responsibility for settling disputes lies ultimately with the will of member governments.) Its procedures were modified and strengthened at the Uruguay Round by the Dispute Settlement Understanding (DSU), which establishes a Dispute Settlement Body (DSB) to administer the rules and procedures of the dispute settlement system. Under the provisions of the DSU, the DSB has "the authority to establish panels, adopt panel and Appellate Body reports, maintain surveillance of implementation of rulings and recommendations and authorise suspension of concessions and other obligations under the covered agreements."[5] One of the central provisions of the DSU reaffirms that members shall not themselves make determinations in trade disputes or suspend concessions but will instead make use of the dispute settlement rules.

The dispute settlement procedure opens with consultations between the parties. The DSU requires a member to enter into consultations within

---

[5] See Article 2(1) DSU

30 days of a request for consultations from another member in order to ascertain whether settlement is possible. If, after 60 days from the request for consultations, there is no settlement, the complaining party may request the establishment of a "panel" to resolve the dispute; or where consultations are denied, the complaining party may move directly to request a panel. Alternatively, the parties may voluntarily agree to follow other means of dispute settlement, including conciliation, mediation and arbitration. These alternative avenues of mediation remain open throughout the dispute settlement procedure.

The function of the panel is to make an objective assessment of the facts of the case and the conformity with the relevant WTO agreement. Its findings will provide the basis for the DSB's recommendations or ruling. Panel procedures are set out in detail in the DSU[6]. A panel should complete its work within 6 months, or, in urgent cases, within 3 months, although this is often not the case. Panel reports may be considered by the DSB for adoption 20 days after they are issued to members. Within 60 days of the report's publication, it will be adopted by the DSB unless the DSB decides by consensus not to adopt the report or one of the parties notifies an intention to appeal.

The concept of appellate review is an important new feature of the DSU. The Appellate Body (AB) is composed of seven members, three of whom will serve on any one case[7]. An appeal to the AB from a panel's finding will be limited to issues of law covered in the panel report. The report of the AB is final, and shall be adopted by the DSB and unconditionally accepted by the parties to the dispute within 30 days of its publication to WTO members, unless the DSB decides by consensus against its adoption.

Once the panel report or the AB report is adopted, the party found to have breached its obligations under a WTO Agreement must notify its

---

[6] Article 8(2) of the DSU provides: "Panel members should be selected with a view to ensuring the independence of the members, a sufficiently diverse background and a wide spectrum of experience."

[7] Members of the AB have to be individuals with recognised standing in the field of law and international trade, and who are not affiliated with any government.

intentions with respect to the implementation of the adopted recommendations or rulings. A time limit is applied and the DSB will keep the implementation under regular review. Further provisions set out rules for compensation or the suspension of concessions in the event of non-implementation by the offending party.

12.5.2 Dispute resolution in practice – the case of hormones in bovine meat[8]

The US-EU hormones dispute was the first trade dispute under the SPS Agreement to be considered by the DSB. It is an important decision, which goes part way to clarifying the concepts of "risk assessment" and "appropriate level of protection", the roles of international standards laid down by the Codex Alimentarius and the precautionary principle.

In 1998, the EU introduced a prohibition on the use of the following six hormonal substances for animal growth promotion: 17β oestradiol, testosterone, progesterone, zeranol, trenbolone acetate, and melengestrol acetate (MGA). The ban applied without discrimination both within the Community and to imports from third countries as from 1 January 1989. It is noteworthy, however, that the EU prohibition was inconsistent with the Codex Alimentarius Guidelines, which authorised the use of these hormones in other countries. As a result of the prohibition, third countries wishing to export bovine meat and meat products to the EU either had to have equivalent legislation or to operate a hormone-free cattle programme.

Some third countries, in particular the US and Canada, contested the legality of the EU hormones ban. The US, in the absence of an agreed solution, applied retaliatory measures in the form of 100% *ad valorem* duties on a variety of EU exports at a cost to EU exporters of about USD93m per year since 1989. In May 1996, these retaliatory measures were suspended when the EU asked the DSB to establish a panel to resolve the lawfulness of the dispute.

---

[8] I am grateful in compiling this account to DG SANCO's regular bulletins on the WTO dispute on hormones in bovine meat.

The DSB established two panels to assess the conformity of the EU prohibition with its WTO obligations under the SPS Agreement. The reports of these panels were delivered in August 1997 and the EU ban was found not to conform with three provisions of the SPS Agreement. The EU appealed the conclusions of the panels in September 1997. In its report of January 1998, the AB reversed two of the three conclusions found by the panels, but upheld the finding that the EU prohibition of imports of meat from hormone-treated animals did not comply with the requirement that such a measure be based on an assessment, "as appropriate to the circumstances", of the risks to human health. It went on to state that it did not consider the risk assessment presented by the EU as sufficient because "it did not focus specifically enough on residues in meat" for the first five hormones and that, for the sixth hormone, MGA, no risk assessment had been performed. The DSB therefore recommended that the EU bring its measures into conformity with its obligations under the SPS Agreement.

Of importance, though, were the AB's conclusions on the scope of the precautionary principle. The AB[9] held that the precautionary principle was reflected in, *but not exhausted by*, Article 5.7 of the SPS Agreement. Article 5.7 provides:

> "In cases where relevant scientific evidence is insufficient, a Member may provisionally adopt sanitary or phytosanitary measures on the basis of available scientific information, including that from the relevant international organisations as well as from sanitary and phytosanitary measures applied by other members. In such circumstances, members shall seek to obtain the additional information necessary for a more objective assessment of risk and review the sanitary or phytosanitary measure accordingly within a reasonable period of time."

---

[9] AB 1997 - 4, para 124, and see also the Communication on the precautionary principle, Annex II

Significantly, the AB also stated that members of the SPS Agreement had the "right to establish their own level of sanitary protection, which level may be higher than that implied in existing international standards, guidelines and recommendations." Furthermore, it accepted that "responsible, representative governments commonly act from perspectives of prudence and precaution where risks of irreversible damage to human health are concerned." To this end the Commission is seeking to achieve within the WTO a universal agreement on the applicability of the precautionary principle.

In May 1998, the DSB awarded the EU 15 months to implement its recommendation. The EU decided to implement the recommendations by carrying out an additional risk assessment in accordance with the findings of both the panels and the AB, but it failed to complete the necessary assessment and subsequent adoption of the recommended risk management measures by 13 May 1999, the deadline for implementation. As a result, the WTO awarded the US and Canada nullification and impairment suspension of concessions, which, in effect, means that the US and Canada are authorised to apply retaliation in the form of 100% *ad valorem* duty on imports on a variety of EC products, again at huge cost to EU exporters.

The EU's response to the findings of the AB had been to commission 17 specific research studies and to instruct the Committee of Veterinary Measures Relating to Public Health (SCVPH) to carry out an assessment of the risk to human health arising from the use of the six hormones as growth promoters in animals and, particularly, the effect of their residues being present in meat destined for the consumer. The SCVPH adopted its final report unanimously on 30 April 1999 and subsequently reconfirmed it on 3 May 2000. It identified a risk to consumers (including possible endocrine, developmental, immunological, neurobiological, immunotoxic, genotoxic and carcinogenic effects) with differing levels of conclusive evidence for each of the substances, but also concluded that the current state of scientific knowledge did not permit a quantitative estimate of the risks to be calculated. In so doing, it criticised the assumptions and studies on which the Joint FAO/WHO Expert Committee on Food Additives advising the

Codex Alimentarius had authorised the use of these hormones for animal growth in other countries. More particularly:-

- It concluded that there was a substantial body of recent and reliable scientific evidence suggesting that 17β oestradiol should be considered as a complete carcinogen (both tumour-initiating and tumour-promoting), although it was not possible to quantify this risk.

- For the hormone MGA there was no available risk assessment; the SCVPH concluded that publicly available information was inadequate to carry out a complete assessment, but that the available data allowed a non-quantifiable risk to consumers to be identified.

- For the other four hormones (testosterone, progesterone, trenbolone acetate and zeranol), it was found that available information was also inadequate to allow a quantitative estimate of the risk but that a risk to consumers had been identified in qualitative terms.

- Significantly, it concluded that, because no safe threshold could be established for any of these hormones, exposure to even small traces in meat carried a risk, and that "of the various susceptible risk groups, pre-pubertal children is the group of greatest concern".

In view of these findings, the Commission has adopted a proposal that seeks to ban definitively the use of 17β oestradiol and its ester-like derivatives in farm animals and to maintain the ban on the other five substances until more complete scientific information becomes available. The proposal is currently being ratified through the co-decision procedure.

By adopting such a proposal, the EU is breaching its requirements to comply with the decision of the DSB of the WTO. However, it finds its justification for doing so in seeking to afford an appropriate level of protection for its citizens. What is still considered to be a trade protectionist measure by the US (now backed up by the (supposedly binding) DSB finding) is nonetheless still considered to be a justified prohibition by the EU on grounds of risk to public health.

12.6   Enlargement

The EU is conducting accession negotiations with Cyprus, Czech Republic, Estonia, Hungary, Poland, Slovenia, Latvia, Lithuania, Malta, Slovakia, Romania and Bulgaria. The first accessions are expected to take place in time for the next European Parliament elections in 2004. It should be understood that each of these candidate EU countries will have to incorporate all relevant legislation concerning EU food law into its domestic law. To this end, the Commission has asked each of the candidate countries to draw up a Food Safety Strategy, which each has produced. The process of enlargement is both difficult and time-consuming, but will, on accession, expand the jurisdiction of EU food law to 12 new Member States[10], some 500 million consumers.

12.7   Conclusion

As can be seen from the example provided by hormone-treated beef, even within the multilateral and supposedly binding framework of the WTO, trade disputes between members are time-consuming to resolve and difficult to enforce. This is not to say that the DSB has not successfully enforced WTO obligations in other disputes. But the decision-making process of the DSB will be severely tested when the restriction on trade is justified on the grounds of risk to human health or the environment and where scientific opinion differs widely, as it often does. It is for this reason that the EU is anxious to achieve agreement within the framework of the WTO for the scope of the precautionary principle when used by decision makers in the management of risk. For the EU, such agreement would allow WTO members to prohibit imports where preliminary objective scientific evaluation indicates that there are reasonable grounds for concern that the effect of a product on human/animal/plant health and the environment would be inconsistent with the high level of protection that, in its own case,

---

[10] The Commission has prepared a paper on food safety and enlargement, which is available from the DG SANCO Web site at: www.europa.eu.int/comm/dgs/health_consumer/enlargement/enlarg_food01_en.

the Community seeks for its consumers. It is for these reasons[11] that the ban on hormone-treated meat, though in violation of a WTO ruling, is still in force within the Community.

---

[11] This is expanded upon in the Commission's Communication on the precautionary principle

APPENDIX I

Action Plan on Food Safety[1]

No.	Action	Objective	Ref. in WP	Adoption by Commission	Adoption by Council/ Parliament
I. Priority measures					
1.	Proposal for setting up a European Food Authority	To set up an independent European Food Authority.	29	September 2000	December 2001
2.	Proposal for laying down procedures in matters of food safety	To introduce a comprehensive safeguard measure covering the whole food chain, including feed.	80	September 2000	December 2001
		To establish a comprehensive Rapid Alert System covering all feed and food emergencies with harmonised requirements and procedures, including third countries on the basis of reciprocity.	18		
3.	Proposal for a General Food Law Directive	To establish food safety as the primary objective of EU food law.	67	September 2000	December 2001
		To lay down the common principles underlying food legislation (in particular: scientific basis, responsibility of producers and suppliers, traceability along the food chain, efficient controls and effective enforcement).			
		To increase transparency, consistency and legal security.			

[1] This action plan does not include all of the on-going actions resulting from the obligations in EU legislation

No.	Action	Objective	Ref. in WP	Adoption by Commission	Adoption by Council/ Parliament
4.	Proposal for a Regulation on official food and feed safety controls	To establish a Community framework for official controls on all food and feed safety aspects along the feed and food chain by:	Ch. 6	December 2000	December 2001
		– merging and completing existing rules for national controls and Community controls and inspections within the EU, at the borders and in third countries.			
		– integrating existing monitoring and surveillance systems so as to establish a comprehensive and effective food safety monitoring and surveillance system from farm to table.			
		– establishing a framework for organising consolidated annual programs for controls of foodstuffs.			
		– merging existing Community rules on mutual assistance and administrative co-operation.			
		– creating a Community approach towards a financial support for official controls.			
5.	Proposal for a Regulation on feed	To establish animal and public health as the primary objective of EU feed legislation	69	December 2001	December 2002
		To lay down common principles underlying feed legislation (in particular: scientific basis, responsibility of producers and suppliers, systematic implementation of hazard analysis and critical control points (HACCP), traceability, efficient controls and enforcement).			
		To recast all existing measures on feedingstuffs so as to create a comprehensive legislative tool increasing transparency, consistency and legal security.			

No.	Action	Objective	Ref. in WP	Adoption by Commission	Adoption by Council/Parliament
6.	Proposal for a Regulation on novel feed	To put into plan a centralised system for the authorisation of use in animal nutrition of non conventional products, in particular of GMOs and GMO derived feedstuffs.	69	September 2000	December 2001
7.	Amendment to the Annex of Directive 96/25/EC on the circulation of feed materials	To amend the definitions of feed materials listed in the Annex to Decision 96/25/EC, particularly with regard to oils and fats and animal products.	69	September 2000	–
8.	Proposal for a Regulation on hygiene	To recast horizontal and vertical Directives on hygiene of food of plant and animal origin. To clarify responsibility of food operators and to introduce the systematic implementation of HACCP. To apply hygiene rules at all levels of the food chain, including primary production.	72	June 2000	June 2000
9.	Amendment to Decision 98/272/EC on epidemio-surveillance of transmissible spongiform encephalopathies (TSEs)	To reinforce TSE surveillance including a study on mandatory testing (rapid post-mortem test) on targeted groups of cattle. To reinforce TSE surveillance in small ruminants	71	March 2000 September 2000	–
10.	Decision on the Member State and third country residue programmes	To ensure efficacy of residue testing in Member States and third countries.	74	December 2000	–
11.	Proposal for amending Directive 89/107/EEC on food additives	To confer implementing powers for maintaining the lists of permitted food additives and to lay down specific provisions in respect of enzymes.	77	December 2000	December 2001

No.	Action	Objective	Ref. in WP	Adoption by Commission	Adoption by Council/Parliament
12.	Proposal for amending Directive 95/2/EC on food additives other than colours and sweeteners	To update and revise the list of food additives other than colours and sweeteners.	77	December 2000	December 2001
13.	Proposal for amending Directive 88/388/EEC on flavourings for use in foodstuffs	To clarify the scope and update definitions, to set maximum limits for toxic substances and to confer implementing powers to the Commission.	77	December 2000	December 2001
14.	Proposal for amending Regulation 258/97 on novel foods and novel food ingredients	To make the necessary adaptations in the light of the conclusions of the report on the implementation of the Regulation and in accordance with the new regulatory framework of Directive 90/220/EEC.	76	December 2001	December 2002
15.	Regulation on the labelling of GMO-free foodstuffs	To give operators the possibility to use labelling claims referring to the absence of use of genetic engineering techniques for the production of foodstuffs.	76 103	September 2000	–
16.	Proposal for amending Directive 79/112/EEC on the labelling, presentation and advertising of foodstuffs	To remove the possibility not to indicate the components of compound ingredients forming less than 25% of the final product and lay down a list of allergenic substances.	100	December 2000	December 2001
17.	Proposals for Commission Directives to fix maximum residue levels (MRLs) of pesticides in food and agricultural commodities	To fix MRLs for pesticides for, inter alia:	74		
		36 pesticides with existing open positions in the residues directives that will automatically go to zero in July 2000 unless the Commission adopts other values		June 2000	–
		To set MRLs at zero for 8 pesticides that were excluded from Annex I to Directive 91/414/EEC		September 2000	

No.	Action	Objective	Ref. in WP	Adoption by Commission	Adoption by Council/Parliament
		To set MRLs for new active substances included in Annex I to Directive 91/414/EEC.		Continuous process	–
18.	Communication on an action plan on nutrition policy	To develop a comprehensive and coherent nutrition policy.	106	December 2000	

II. Feedingstuffs

No.	Action	Objective	Ref. in WP	Adoption by Commission	Adoption by Council/Parliament
19.	Proposal for amending Directive 70/524/EEC concerning additives in feedingstuffs	To consolidate the Directive. To fix maximum residue limits for additives. To clarify certain aspects of the procedure (evaluation reports) and the authorisation (generic versus specific).	69	July 2001	December 2002
20.	Amendment to Decision 91/516/EEC on the list of ingredients the use of which is forbidden in compound feedingstuffs	To introduce the changes deemed necessary to the list of feed materials the use of which must be prohibited in compound feedingstuffs, with particular reference to certain by-products from fat processing.	69	June 2000	–
21.	Amendment to the Annex of Directive 1999/29/EC on the undesirable substances and products in animal nutrition	To fix the maximum limits of dioxins for oils and fats, and for other or all feed materials. To collect information on background contamination of PCB and dioxin-like PCB, MRLs for other potential contaminants of feedingstuffs will also be fixed.	69	December 2000	–
22.	Proposal for amending Directive 96/25/EEC on the circulation of feed materials	Following reflection to decide whether an exclusive positive list of authorised feed materials should be established.	69	December 2002	December 2003

No.	Action	Objective	Ref. in WP	Adoption by Commission	Adoption by Council/Parliament
23.	Proposal for amending Directive 95/53/EEC fixing the principles governing the organisation of official inspections in the field of animal nutrition	To foresee a legal basis for a safeguard clause in case of appearing or spreading hazards related to feedingstuffs likely to pose a risk to human health. To introduce an obligation for Member States to carry out a monitoring programme for contaminants in feedingstuffs. To introduce a Rapid Alert System for feed to be integrated in the Rapid Alert System for food. (to be integrated in action 2)	69	March 2000	March 2001
24.	Proposal for amending Directive 79/373/EEC on the marketing of compound feedingstuffs	To review current provisions for the labelling of compound feedingstuffs.	69	January 2000	March 2001
25.	Proposal for amending Directive 95/69/EEC laying down the conditions and arrangements for approving and registration of certain establishments and intermediaries operating in the feedingstuffs sector	To introduce provisions for: – Approval or registration of manufacturers of compound feedingstuffs – Approval of manufacturers of certain feed materials – Improving traceability of feed materials and identification of critical points – Establishing a code for good manufacturing practice for animal feeding	69	December 2000	December 2001

No.	Action	Objective	Ref. in WP	Adoption by Commission	Adoption by Council/ Parliament
III. Zoonoses					
26.	Proposal for amending Directive 92/117/EEC on zoonoses	To improve monitoring and reporting system for diseases transmissible from animals to man and to reduce prevalence of specified zoonoses (e.g. salmonella).	70	June 2000	June 2000
27.	Decision on Member State and third country programmes for the control of zoonotic agents on animal products exported to the Community	To ensure that Member States implement adequate measures to control zoonotic agents. To ensure that third country products are controlled to the same level as Community products.	70	December 2002	–
IV. Animal health					
28.	Proposal for a Regulation on animal health requirements for products of animal origin	To recast existing animal health rules for products of animal origin.	70	June 2000	June 2002
29.	Increase budgetary allocation for actions provided for in Council Decision 90/424/EEC on expenditure in the veterinary field	To enable actions necessary to improve animal disease eradication (brucellosis, tuberculosis, etc.) To create a task force for monitoring disease eradication in the Member States.	70	May 2000	December 2000
V. Animal by-products					
30.	Proposal for amending Directives 90/667/EEC and 92/118/EEC on animal waste and derived products	To recast existing measures of animal by-products not destined for human consumption (meat and bone meal, rendered fats, manure, etc.)	69	June 2000	December 2001

No.	Action	Objective	Ref. in WP	Adoption by Commission	Adoption by Council/ Parliament
		To ensure that only animal by-products derived from animals declared fit for human consumption can enter the animal feed chain.			
		To clarify responsibility of animal by-products operators.			
		To tighten up official control and to improve traceability.			
VI. BSE/TSE					
31.	Decision on classification according to BSE status	Classification of individual countries in view of changes in BSE status (post-mortem tests).	71	June 2000	–
32.	Amendment to Decision 94/381 (feed ban)	To amend the Decision in the light of recent scientific opinions.	71	March 2000	–
	Decision on the removal of specified risk materials (SRMs) replacing Decision 97/534/EC	To replace Decision 97/534/EC laying down the rules on the prohibition of the use of materials that present risks as regards TSEs. Amendment of the TSE framework proposal accordingly.			
33.	Decision on the harmonisation of BSE rules for imports of live animals and products from third countries	To harmonise the BSE import rules for other third countries.	71	September 2000	–
VII. Hygiene					
34.	Report on the testing of residues in Member States and third countries	To evaluate the performance of national and third country residue programmes.	74	December 2000	–

No.	Action	Objective	Ref. in WP	Adoption by Commission	Adoption by Council/ Parliament
35.	Modification of the Annex to Council Directive 96/23/EC on residue monitoring	To re-enforce the monitoring and detection of PCBs and dioxins in food of animal origin.	74	June 2000	–
36.	Proposal for a Decision to review the ante- and post-mortem procedures for animals and meat	To make ante- and post-mortem inspections risk based, and to review inspection methods applied at present.	72	September 2001	December 2002
37.	Decision on microbiological standards on certain foods	To fix the maximum limits of undesirable micro-organisms in foodstuffs, after risk assessment.	72	December 2001	–
VIII. Contaminants					
38.	Amendment to Regulation No 194/97 setting maximum limits for certain contaminants	To set up limits for several contaminants: ochratoxin A, cadmium, lead, 3-MCPD, dioxin and, possibly, PCBs.	73	December 2000	–
IX. Food additives and flavourings					
39.	Report on the intake of food additives	To provide an overview of the intake of food additives in the European Union.	77	June 2000	–
40.	Proposal for amending Directive 94/35/EC on sweeteners	To update and revise the list of sweeteners for use in foodstuffs.	77	December 2000	December 2001
41.	Amendment to Directives 95/31/EC, 95/45/EC and 96/77/EC on purity criteria for food additives (including sweeteners and colours)	To introduce a general requirement for a new safety evaluation for permitted additives made from new sources or with new methods.	77	September 2000	–

No.	Action	Objective	Ref. in WP	Adoption by Commission	Adoption by Council/ Parliament
42.	Amendment to Directive 81/712/EEC laying down Community methods of analysis for the respect of purity criteria	To replace existing provisions with a set of general principles and a reference to other similar provisions.	77	June 2001	–
43.	Decision amending the Community register of flavouring substances used in or on foodstuffs	To update the register.	77	December 2000	–
44.	Regulation establishing a programme for the evaluation of flavouring substances	To set priorities and time limits for evaluation.	77	June 2000	–
45.	Proposal for a Regulation on additives used in flavourings	To lay down a list of additives authorised for use in flavourings.	77	June 2001	December 2002
46.	Proposal for a Regulation on smoke flavourings	To lay down the conditions for the production of smoke flavourings.	77	June 2001	December 2002
X. Materials in contact with food					
47.	Proposal for amending Directive 89/109/EEC on food contact materials	To allow the update of specific Directives through regulatory procedure and to change or add provisions on the labelling of contact materials.	78	December 2000	December 2001
48.	Amendment to Directive 90/128/EEC on food contact plastics	To update the list of authorised food contact plastics.	78	December 2000	–
49.	Practical guide on food contact materials	To provide guidance on the application of Community provisions relating to contact materials.	78	December 2000	–

No.	Action	Objective	Ref. in WP	Adoption by Commission	Adoption by Council/ Parliament
XI. Novel foods/Genetically modified organisms					
50.	Regulation clarifying the authorisation procedure for novel foods and novel food ingredients	To clarify and make more transparent the procedure laid down in Regulation 258/97 for the authorisation of novel foods and novel food ingredients.	76	September 2000	–
51.	Report on the implementation of Regulation 258/97 on novel foods and novel food ingredients	To examine the application of the "novel food" legislation and assess its impact on public health, consumer protection and information, and the functioning of the internal market.	76	December 2001	–
52.	Regulation on the labelling of food containing or derived from genetically modified organisms	To further harmonise the provisions governing the labelling of food, additives and flavourings containing or derived from GMO material.	76 103	September 2000	–
XII. Irradiation of food					
53.	Proposal for amending Directive 1999/3/EC on foods and food ingredients treated by irradiation	To complete the Community list of foods and food ingredients which may be treated with ionising radiation.	79	December 2000	June 2002
54.	Decision establishing the list of irradiation facilities	Publication of the list of irradiation facilities authorised in the Member States and those in third countries which have been approved by the EU.	79	December 2000	–
XIII. Dietetic foods/food supplements/fortified foods					
55.	Directive on foods intended for intense muscular effort	To lay down specific provisions for foods intended to meet the expenditure of intense muscular effort, especially by sportsmen.	105	December 2001	–

187

No.	Action	Objective	Ref. in WP	Adoption by Commission	Adoption by Council/Parliament
56.	Report on foods intended for persons suffering from diabetes	To assess the need for specific provisions for food for people with carbohydrate-metabolism disorders.	105	December 2001	–
57.	Proposal for amending Directive 89/398/EEC on dietetic foods	To define the conditions for making the claims "low-sodium" or "sodium-free", and "gluten-free".	105	December 2001	December 2002
58.	Directive on purity criteria for nutritional substances in food for particular nutritional use	To lay down purity criteria for nutritional substances which are added to food for particular nutritional use or which are present in food supplements and foods to which nutrients are added.	105	December 2002	–
59.	Directive on substances added for nutritional purposes in foods for particular nutritional uses	To establish a positive list of the various substances which may be added for nutritional purposes in foods for particular nutritional uses.	105	June 2000	–
60.	Proposal for a Directive on food supplements	To lay down common criteria for marketing concentrated source of nutrients (vitamins and minerals).	105	March 2000	March 2001
61.	Proposal for a Directive on fortified foods	To lay down provisions for marketing foods to which nutrients such as vitamins and minerals have been added.	105	September 2000	September 2001
62.	Amendment to Directive 91/321/EEC on infant formulae and follow-on formulae	To set up a list of pesticides not to be used in agricultural products intended for use in these formulae.	105	November 2000	–
63.	Amendment to Directive 96/5/EEC on processed baby foods	To set up a list of pesticides not to be used in agricultural products intended for infants and young children.	105	November 2000	–

No.	Action	Objective	Ref. in WP	Adoption by Commission	Adoption by Council/ Parliament
64.	Amendment to Directive 80/777/EEC on mineral waters	To lay down a list of constituents of mineral waters and the conditions of use for the treatment of certain mineral waters with ozone enriched air.	79	September 2000	–
XIV. Labelling of food					
65.	Proposal for amending Directive 79/112/EEC on the labelling, presentation and advertising of foodstuffs	To specify the conditions under which "functional claims" and "nutritional claims" may be made.	101	July 2001	July 2002
66.	Proposal for amending Directive on nutrition labelling	To bring the provisions on nutrition labelling into line with consumer needs and expectations.	101	July 2001	July 2002
67.	Proposal for amending Directive on misleading advertising	To clarify the scope of the Directive with regard to claims concerning in particular food, health and the environment.	102	December 2000	July 2002
XV. Pesticides					
68.	Regulation on monitoring of pesticide residues in food	To improve co-ordination and quality of monitoring of pesticides in foods.	74	March 2000	–
69.	Recommendation for a co-ordinated Community Monitoring Programme for pesticides residues in Foods for the year 2001	Recommendation for a co-ordinated Community Monitoring Programme for pesticides residues in Foods for the year 2001.	74	December 2000	–

No.	Action	Objective	Ref. in WP	Adoption by Commission	Adoption by Council/Parliament
70.	Commission Decisions for pesticide active substances including in or excluding from Annex I to Directive 91/414/EEC	Pesticides active substances evaluated in the framework of Directive 91/414/EEC need, after the evaluation to be either included in Annex I or withdrawn from the market.	74	Continuous process	–
71.	Regulation on the evaluation of existing pesticides active substances	To fix a priority list of substances for evaluation at Community level; to introduce a notification procedure for all remaining substances.	74	December 2000	–
		To lay out the ground rules for the final stage of the Community evaluation of active substances.		September 2001	
72.	Proposal for amending Directive 91/414/EEC	*Inter alia*, to – extend competence to include genetically modified organisms, – allow a harmonised Community regime to charge fees for the evaluation of new pesticides active substances – develop a fast-track procedure for low-risk substances, – clarify problems relating to data protection, work-sharing, parallel imports, classification and labelling, borderlines with biocides legislation, etc.	74	June 2002	June 2003
73.	Directive to develop and adopt the Annexes to Directive 91/414/EEC	To develop Community data requirements for non-GMO microbial plant protection products	74	December 2000	–
		To develop a harmonised set of risk and safety phrases		December 2001	

No.	Action	Objective	Ref. in WP	Adoption by Commission	Adoption by Council/Parliament
		To establish uniform principles for assessment of safety of micro-organisms as plant protection products.		December 2001	
XVI. Nutrition					
74.	Proposal for Council Recommendations on European dietary guidelines	To support the Member States in their development of nutrition policy at the national level.	107	December 2000	December 2001
		To streamline the flow of information to enable consumers to make informed choices.			
XVII. Seeds					
75.	Proposal for a Regulation concerning environmental risk assessment in respect of genetically modified plant varieties	To lay down the specific conditions for the conduct of the risk assessment applicable to genetically modified varieties of agricultural and vegetable plant species, as required under Council Directive 98/95/EC, as required under Council Directive 98/95/EC.	69 76	March 2001	March 2002
76.	Directives on environmental risk assessment and the assessment principles laid down in Regulation 258/97, in respect of genetically modified plant varieties	To provide for technical and scientific guidance for the conduct of the assessment applicable to genetically modified varieties of agricultural and vegetable plant species.	69 76	June 2001	–
77.	Directives amending the Annexes of the Directives on the marketing of seeds	To lay down the details of the labelling requirement as established by Council Directive 98/95/EC for seeds of genetically modified plant varieties of agricultural and vegetable plant species.	69 76	December 2000	–

No.	Action	Objective	Ref. in WP	Adoption by Commission	Adoption by Council/ Parliament
		To lay down the growing conditions and other requirements for purity concerning the adventitious presence of genetically modified seeds in seed lots of traditional plant varieties.			
78.	Proposal for a Directive amending Directive 68/193/EEC on the marketing of material for the vegetative propagation of the vine.	To lay down assessment procedures and labelling requirements for propagating material of genetically modified varieties of the vine.	69 76	January 2000	June 2001
XVIII. Supporting measures					
79.	Proposal for a Regulation on the financial support for food safety actions at Community level	To provide for a uniform legal basis to ensure adequate Community financial support of actions necessary to enhance food safety (liaison and reference laboratories, exchange of officials, training of officials, etc.)	Ch. 3	December 2000	December 2001
80.	Proposal for a Decision establishing a database of dietary intakes across the whole EU population.	To create a basis of exposure data used in risk assessments and nutrition.	74	December 2000	December 2001
81.	Decision on an Advisory Committee on Food Safety	To improve involvement of all stakeholders in the Community food safety policy by streamlining the existing Advisory Committees.	11	December 2000	–
XIX. Third country policy/international relations					
82.	Proposals for agreements with third countries	To establish further agreements with third countries on veterinary and/or phyto-sanitary issues.	113	Continuous process	–

No.	Action	Objective	Ref. in WP	Adoption by Commission	Adoption by Council/ Parliament
83.	Proposal for accession of the European Community to Codex Alimentarius	To reinforce the participation of the European Union in the elaboration of international food standards.	111	May 2000	December 2000
84.	Proposal for accession of the European Community to OIE	To reinforce the participation of the European Union in the elaboration of international animal health standards.	111	December 2000	December 2001

193

APPENDIX II

Co-decision Procedure

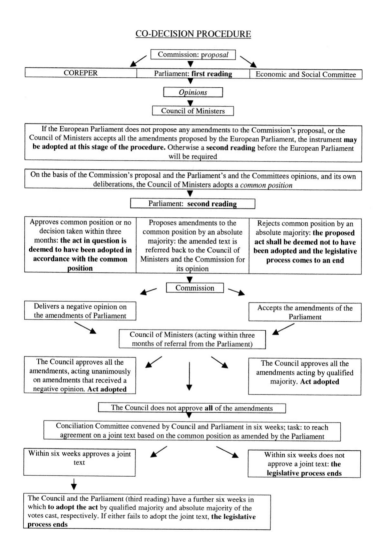

CO-DECISION PROCEDURE

Commission: *proposal*

COREPER | Parliament: **first reading** | Economic and Social Committee

Opinions

Council of Ministers

If the European Parliament does not propose any amendments to the Commission's proposal, or the Council of Ministers accepts all the amendments proposed by the European Parliament, the instrument **may be adopted at this stage of the procedure.** Otherwise a **second reading** before the European Parliament will be required

On the basis of the Commission's proposal and the Parliament's and the Committees opinions, and its own deliberations, the Council of Ministers adopts a *common position*

Parliament: **second reading**

| Approves common position or no decision taken within three months: **the act in question is deemed to have been adopted in accordance with the common position** | Proposes amendments to the common position by an absolute majority: the amended text is referred back to the Council of Ministers and the Commission for its opinion | Rejects common position by an absolute majority: **the proposed act shall be deemed not to have been adopted and the legislative process comes to an end** |

Commission

| Delivers a negative opinion on the amendments of Parliament | | Accepts the amendments of the Parliament |

Council of Ministers (acting within three months of referral from the Parliament)

| The Council approves all the amendments, acting unanimously on amendments that received a negative opinion. **Act adopted** | | The Council approves all the amendments acting by qualified majority. **Act adopted** |

The Council does not approve **all** of the amendments

Conciliation Committee convened by Council and Parliament in six weeks; task: to reach agreement on a joint text based on the common position as amended by the Parliament

| Within six weeks approves a joint text | | Within six weeks does not approve a joint text: **the legislative process ends** |

The Council and the Parliament (third reading) have a further six weeks in which **to adopt the act** by qualified majority and absolute majority of the votes cast, respectively. If either fails to adopt the joint text, **the legislative process ends**

APPENDIX III

National Food Authorities of Member States and Candidate Countries

Member States	Contact details
Austria	Federal Ministry of Agriculture Forestry Environment and Water Management Stubenring 1 A-1012 Vienna Tel: + 43 1 711 00-0 Web site: http://webred.lfrz.at
Belgium	Federal Agency for the Safety of the Food Chain Service Information WTC III – 17th Floor Boulevard Simon Bolivar B-1000 Brussels Tel: +32 2 208 4535 Fax: + 32 2 208 4540
Denmark	Ministry of Food, Agriculture and Fisheries Holbersgade 2 DK – 1057 Copenhagen K Denmark Tel: +45 33 92 33 01 Fax: + 45 33 14 50 42 E-mail: fvm@fvm.dk Web site: www.fvm.dk

Finland	Ministry of Agriculture and Forestry PO Box 30 Fin – 00023 Government Helsinki Tel: +358 9 16001 Fax: +358 9 1605 4202 Web site: www.mmm.fi
France	Ministry of Agriculture, Food, Fisheries and Rural Affairs 78 Rue de Varenne 75349 Paris 07SP Tel: + 33 1 49 55 49 55 E-mail: webmaster@agriculture.gouv.fr Web site: www.agriculture.gouv.fr
Germany	Ministry of Consumer Protection, Food and Agriculture Postfach 14 02 70 53107 Bonn Tel: + 01888-529-4262 Fax: + 01888-529-4262 E-mail: internet@bmvel.bund.de Web site: www.verbraucherministerium.de
Greece	Ministry of Agriculture Acharnon 5 Athens 104 32 Tel: 0102124000 Web site: www.minagric.gr

Ireland   Department of Agriculture and Food
Agriculture House
Kildare Street
Dublin 2
Tel: 1890 200 509
Web site: www.irlgov.ie/daff

Italy   Ministry of Agriculture and Forestry
Via XX Settembre n. 20
00187 Rome
Tel: 06 46651
Fax: 4742314
Web site: www.politicheagricole.it

Luxembourg   Ministry of Agriculture
1, Rue de la Congregation
L – 1352 Luxembourg
Tel: + 352 478 25 00
Fax: +352 46 40 27
E-mail: info@sip.etat.lu
Web site: www.gouvernement.lu

Netherlands   Ministry of Agriculture, Nature Management and
Fisheries
Postbus 20401
NL-2500 EK Den Haag
Tel: + 31 70 3786868
Fax: +31 70 3786123
E-mail: pbih@ih.agro.nl
Web site: www.minlnv.nl

Portugal

Ministry of Agriculture, Rural Affairs and Fisheries
Av. Conde Valbom
98 – 1050 Lisbon
Tel: + 21 798 36 00
Fax: + 21 798 38 34
E-mail: geral@min-agricultura.pt
Web site: www.min-agricultura.pt

Spain

Ministry of Agriculture, Fisheries and Food
Web site: www.mapya.es

Sweden

Ministry of Agriculture, Food and Fisheries
Fredsgatan 8
SE – 103 33 Stockholm
Tel: + 46 8 405 10 00
Fax: + 46 8 20 64 96
Web site: http://jordbruk.regeringen.se

United Kingdom

Department for Environment, Food and Rural Affairs
Nobel House
17 Smith Square
London SW1P 3JR
Tel: +44 207 238 6951 (Helpline)
Fax: +44 207 238 3329
Web site: www.defra.gov.uk

Candidate Countries	Contact details
Czech Republic	Ministry of Agriculture Tènov 17 Prague Tel: + 420 2 2181 2216 Fax: + 420 2181 2940 Web site: www.mze.cz
Cyprus	Ministry of Agriculture, Natural Resources and Environment Press and Information Office Apellis St 1456 Lrfkosia (Nicosia) Tel: + 3572 22801198 Fax: +3572 22666123 E-mail: pioxx@cytanet.com.cy Web site: www.pio.gov.cy
Estonia	Department of Veterinary and Food Lai 39/41 15056 Tallinn Tel: (0) 625 6101 Fax: (0) 625 6200 E-mail: pm@agri.ee Web site: www.agri.ee
Hungary	Department of Food Industry Web site: www.fvm.hu
Latvia	Ministry of Agriculture Republikas laukums 2 Riga LV-1981 Tel: 7027010 Fax: 7027250 Web site: www.zm.gov.lv

Lithuania	Ministry of Agriculture Gedimino Av. 19 (Lelevelio 6) LT-2025 Vilnius Tel: +370 5 2391001 Fax: 5 2391212 Web site: http://terra.zum.lt/min
Malta	Ministry of Agriculture and Fisheries Barriera Wharf Valletta – CMR 02 Tel: 21 255 125 Fax: 21 231 805 E-mail: peter-paul.bonnici@gov.mt Web site: www.doi.gov.mt
Poland	Department of Agri-Food Processing and Agricultural Markets Wspólna Street No. 30 00-930 Warsaw Tel: + 48 22 623 10 00 E-mail: webmaster@minrol.gov.pl Web site: www.mintol.gov.pl
Slovakia	Ministry of Agriculture Dobroviova 12 Bratislava 812 66 11 Tel: +421 2 592 66 11 Fax: + 421 2 529 68 510 E-mail: majkut@mpsr.sanet.sk Web site: www.mpsr.sk
Slovenia	Ministry of Agriculture Dunajaska 56, 58 1000 Lubiljana Tel: + 386 1 478 9000 Fax: + 386 1 478 9021 E-mail: gp.mkgp@gov.si Web site: www.sigov.si/mkgp/Pslo